SURVIVORS CLUB

MICHAEL BORNSTEIN
AND DEBBIE BORNSTEIN HOLINSTAT

SURVIVORS CLUB

THE TRUE STORY OF A VERY YOUNG
PRISONER OF AUSCHWITZ

SQUARE
FISH

FARRAR STRAUS GIROUX | NEW YORK

FOR ISRAEL AND SAMUEL BORNSTEIN

🚩
SQUARE
FISH

An imprint of Macmillan Publishing Group, LLC
175 Fifth Avenue, New York, NY 10010
mackids.com

SURVIVORS CLUB. Copyright © 2017 by Michael Bornstein
and Debbie Bornstein Holinstat.
All rights reserved. Printed in the United States of America by
LSC Communications, Harrisonburg, Virginia.

Square Fish and the Square Fish logo are trademarks of Macmillan and
are used by Farrar Straus Giroux under license from Macmillan.

Our books may be purchased in bulk for promotional, educational, or business use.
Please contact your local bookseller or the Macmillan Corporate and Premium
Sales Department at (800) 221-7945 ext. 5442 or by email
at MacmillanSpecialMarkets@macmillan.com.

Library of Congress Cataloging-in-Publication Data

Names: Bornstein, Michael, 1940– author.
Title: Survivors club : the true story of a very young prisoner of Auschwitz /
    Michael Bornstein, Debbie Bornstein Holinstat.
Description: New York : Farrar Straus Giroux Books for Young Readers, [2017]
Identifiers: LCCN 2016028010 (print) | LCCN 2016028539 (ebook) |
    ISBN 978-0-374-30571-0 (hardback) | ISBN 978-1-250-11875-2 (paperback) |
    ISBN 978-0-374-30572-7 (ebook)
Subjects: LCSH: Bornstein, Michael, 1940– —Juvenile literature. |
    Jews—Poland—Żarki—Biography—Juvenile literature. | Jewish children in
    the Holocaust—Poland—Żarki—Biography—Juvenile literature. | Auschwitz
    (Concentration camp)—Juvenile literature. | Holocaust, Jewish
    (1939–1945)—Poland—Żarki—Personal narratives—Juvenile literature. |
    Żarki (Poland)—Biography—Juvenile literature. | BISAC: JUVENILE
    NONFICTION / History / Holocaust. | JUVENILE NONFICTION /
    History / Military & Wars.
Classification: LCC DS 134.72.B684 A3 2017 (print) | LCC DS 134.72.B684
    (ebook) | DDC 940.53/18092 [B] —dc23
LC record available at https://lccn.loc.gov/2016028010

Originally published in the United States by Farrar Straus Giroux
First Square Fish edition, 2019
Book designed by Andrew Arnold
Square Fish logo designed by Filomena Tuosto

7 9 10 8

AR: 6.3 / LEXILE: 890L

CONTENTS

PREFACE

IT'S TIME TO TALK

MICHAEL BORNSTEIN

That's me in the photo—the little kid in front on the right. As a four-year-old boy, I managed to evade death in a murder mill where more than one million Jews were killed during the Holocaust. I was one of the youngest prisoners to exit the Auschwitz death camp alive.

This picture is taken from movies made by the Soviet army after they liberated Auschwitz on January 27, 1945. Nowadays, you can easily find snippets from these films online. In the image, I am with a group of children and we are showing the cameraman the inmate numbers tattooed on our arms when we arrived at the camp. Of the 2,819 inmates freed by the Russians, only 52 were under the age of eight.

For a very long time, I didn't talk about what happened to me during the war. People assumed I kept silent because it was too traumatic to discuss. It's true—I don't like to think about such awful things. When people notice my tattoo, B-1148, I mention Auschwitz—but I never dwell on that place.

There's another reason, though. I've always known that I had a story to tell, but for the longest time I was scared to talk, because whatever I say becomes a part of the written record of World War II and I don't want to get anything wrong. My memories from that period come in and out like a cascade of images, some clear, some fuzzy. There are times I'll catch a glimpse of a distant, tragic episode—and then the image fades away.

People have told me, "It's better you don't remember." But how would you like it if you couldn't recall what your own brother looked like? For most of my life, I couldn't even answer the most basic question: How did I survive for six months at a camp known for killing children on arrival? How did I miss the "Death March" that cleared the camp of sixty thousand prisoners just a few days before Soviet troops arrived?

I finally know.

Not too long ago, I traveled to Israel to visit the Yad Vashem Holocaust Remembrance Museum, where a document is stored with my very name on it. This was a document written and saved by Soviet soldiers. The day I learned what my own records showed, I knew my survival proves that miracles happen in the smallest and most unlikely of ways.

For much of my life, I didn't even know images of me at Auschwitz existed. The first time I realized I was one of the children in these Soviet films, I was stunned. It was a coincidental discovery I'll share at the end of this book. I recently found something else shocking, too. One afternoon, I went looking online for the image of myself during my liberation from Auschwitz. I did a Google search and found my picture without much difficulty. Then I clicked on the "Visit page" button displayed next to the image and was taken to a website dedicated to claims that the Holocaust is a lie—that it never happened at all! My photo was being manipulated on a website for people who wanted to warp history. Somebody had captioned my photo with a claim that it shows Jews lied when they said that the young were killed on arrival in Auschwitz, or when they said that Auschwitz was anything worse than a labor camp.

Incredibly, scores of visitors on the site had left comments, agreeing that Auschwitz couldn't have been such a bad place. They pointed to my image and several others of child survivors to show how "healthy" we all looked the day we were freed. (In fact, the films were taken a couple of days after liberation. We had been bundled up in many layers of clothing against the cold, and in the movie some of us are wearing adult prison uniforms as well.)

I slammed my computer shut in disgust. I was horrified. My hands shook with anger. But now I'm almost grateful for the sighting. It made me realize that if we survivors remain silent—if we don't gather the resolve to share our stories—then the only voices left to hear will be those of the liars and the bigots.

I was finally compelled to talk, only I'm not a writer. I'm a scientist. So I turned to the third of my four children, Debbie Bornstein Holinstat, a television news producer who had often told me that my story needed to be documented. I decided to put the pen in her hand and do whatever I could to guide her in writing my story.

Finally, with Debbie's help, I am letting go of the stories my relatives and I kept tightly padlocked in our minds for more than half a century. It is time.

DEBBIE BORNSTEIN HOLINSTAT

When I was little, I never really thought much about the tattoo of numbers on my dad's forearm. It was just part of his skin. It was always there. Sometimes in summer when short sleeves are a must, strangers would notice it and ask, "Where'd you get that?"

"Auschwitz. I'm not from around here," he'd say with a laugh. Then he'd immediately turn his attention back to whatever he was doing. Good luck to anyone who tried to get more information!

When my sisters, brother, and I each respectively reached about fifth grade, we started asking our father questions, too, with only marginally better results. If we pressed him, he would maybe share one beastly, heartbreaking memory. We'd ask for more information.

"I don't know, Debbie," he'd say. "I was really young. I'm not always sure how to separate what I remember, and what I *think* I remember." We heard that answer a lot. Then we'd visit one of his cousins, and a story would slip. We'd overhear him talking to our mom, and another story would slip. An older relative would take the microphone to give a toast at a family wedding, and yet another piece of the puzzle was added. Slowly, and in pieces, we four kids grew up learning anecdotes that were woven into the fabric of our being. Like the tattoo on my dad's arm, a lot of those stories were just always there—rarely mentioned but always there.

When I hit my twenties and became a TV news writer,

I started to think about putting my father's stories all down in a book. The timing still wasn't right, though. "I don't know, Debala—maybe someday," my father would say.

Then, suddenly, seventy years after he was freed from Auschwitz, I was stunned to hear my father say, "You know something? I think we should do this." Of course that meant that I was now the person who had to bear the weight of accuracy and detail on her shoulders. *Ah! What did I get myself into?*

When I saw the website that used my dad's photo to try to manipulate history, though—that gave me fuel to get the job done. For every forum telling lies about the Holocaust today, let there be a hundred more that tell the truth.

Anxious to fill in every detail my father could not, I went into journalist mode. He had been imprisoned in the Jewish ghetto in his family's hometown of Żarki, Poland, and then transported to Auschwitz. I spoke with those who knew my father's relatives before and after the war. Museums and genealogy centers from Washington, D.C., to Warsaw generously helped me uncover paperwork that solved more mysteries. I listened to old tape recordings of my grandmother Sophie, and slowly all of the fractured pieces of information I'd been given as I grew up fell into place.

My dad mentioned the stunning find from Yad Vashem that solved the biggest mystery in his survival. It was a document that even museum curators said they were shocked to discover. But there was much more to be found. A collection of essays printed in Hebrew told stories of Israel Bornstein, my dad's papa, a man my father always wished he could remember more clearly, but never more so than when we read accounts of his unbelievable acts of heroism. The essays were written by survivors from the family's small hometown. You'll soon learn why everyone in Żarki knew Israel Bornstein by name. Also, my father and I made use of a diary graciously shared with us by the family of one townsman who was in hiding with relatives at a farmhouse bunker. That diary was shared with us privately, and it contains crucial background information on the town and the treatment of Jews there before and after the invasion.

Now, more than seven decades after my father walked out of Auschwitz in front of Soviet cameras, the family's story can finally be told, with a comforting certainty about the facts of his survival. As my father and I worked to uncover the true story of what happened to the family during the Holocaust, we tried to keep this book as honest as possible. While the underlying events are entirely factual, there is some fiction here: conversations had to be imagined, thoughts and feelings projected, certain names changed, and some minor details adjusted to put this into narrative form.

For instance, in the opening scene of our story, we can say with absolute certainty that German soldiers barged into the family's home just weeks after Germany's invasion of Poland in September 1939. While we may be able to make only an educated guess as to the color of the dress my grandmother was wearing in this scene—or what exactly she said—we know that the soldiers, like a band of thieving pirates, demanded money and helped themselves to whatever treasure they desired. It is also true that in the moments leading up to the soldiers' arrival, Israel Bornstein managed to hide some of the family's belongings. Among the items was one small but special religious relic. It didn't look like much—but it represented a lot.

SURVIVORS CLUB

1

REMEMBER THE CUP

"Sophie, keep Samuel with you and watch through the window," Papa called to Mamishu, my mother. "Do not move."

Papa grabbed a burlap sack and raced from the kitchen to the bedroom, filling the bag with silver picture frames, some crystal, my mother's pearls, and many gold coins.

It was October 1939, and German soldiers were coming to my family's gray limestone house on Sosnawa Street in Żarki, Poland.

Mamishu stood by the living room window as daylight was beginning to dim outside and tapped her index finger nervously against my older brother Samuel's small, dimpled hand. Her other hand rested on her swollen belly, where I was still in a blissful state of coming into being.

"Israel, we should have thought of this sooner! It's too

late. Just put it all under our bed and let's hope they don't check there. You're acting crazy!"

"I know exactly what I'm doing, Sophie. Just stay right there and tell me when they get close."

When I heard about this scene years later, I was always told that Papa spoke with a voice so soothing, it hardly matched the frantic movements Mamishu could see reflected in the window.

Through the glass she was watching packs of German soldiers, neat yet chilling in their button-front uniforms, tall black boots, and matching red armbands with a spider-like symbol inside a white circle. Every soldier carried a sidearm or a rifle slung over his shoulder. The troops marched into our neighbors' houses, coming out minutes later with piles of furs, leather coats, and jewelry-filled pillowcases draped over their arms.

Four-year-old Samuel buried his face into the folds of Mamishu's layered peach-colored skirt each time a gunshot rang out from inside a neighbor's home.

The soldiers were only three houses away now, and Mamishu looked nervously from the front door to the back as my father raced about the house. Bobeshi—that's the Yiddish endearment the family used for Grandma Dora, my father's mother, with whom we lived—sat watching the scene from the sofa.

Earlier that day, German soldiers had announced they would be going door-to-door that afternoon and ordered Jewish residents to be prepared to hand over whatever valuables Germany's Nazi (short for National Socialist) government requested. Under normal circumstances you would call it robbery. The German invaders, however, insisted it was a Jew's responsibility to contribute to the Third Reich (the name the Nazis used for their regime) and help make it richer and stronger.

In our house there would have been plenty to steal. Papa was an accountant and had always been careful to save his money. That day, when soldiers began taking "contributions," Papa was hell-bent on protecting what we had.

"If you're so determined to do this, at least remember the cup!" Mamishu called softly, her eyes still trained out the living room window.

"I've already got it," Papa said, ducking out into the backyard as soldiers' voices grew louder and closer.

From the back door, he counted his steps in Yiddish: *"Eyn, tsvey, dray, fir, finef, zeks . . ."* He stopped at a soft spot in the soil and dug with his hands until his fingers were black with dirt. To a passerby, he would have looked like a man planting bulbs in the fall and looking forward to a spring of blossoms. I guess you could say my father *was* planting. He was burying our family's seeds of hope.

Within a minute, a hidden cavity appeared—a hole reinforced with a piece of scrap metal Papa had bent into a cylindrical shape. It was a makeshift vault, into which he dropped the sack with all our valuables—including one small unadorned silver cup, called a kiddush cup, which is used on Shabbat (the Sabbath). That's a holy day celebrated every week in Jewish homes from sundown Friday to sundown Saturday. It's marked by prayer, wine, and song. Shabbat is intended to be a time of rest and the most peaceful day of the week. The kiddush cup is raised in gratitude.

But there hadn't been much to sing about or celebrate in Żarki since the invasion—especially for Jews. Everything had changed in a matter of weeks.

Jews could not ride buses, and Jewish children weren't allowed to go to school anymore. The Nazis shut down or took over most Jewish businesses. A strict 8:00 p.m. curfew was enforced; anyone caught outside after curfew was arrested or killed. Jews were forced to wear white bands around their arms with a blue six-point Star of David on them so that everyone would know who was Jewish.

When Nazi soldiers banged at the door, Mamishu let out a strange screech—like a scream that was strangled by fear.

She had meant to calmly say *Come in*, but of course pleasantries weren't necessary. The door was pushed open before Mamishu even found her voice.

Please appear, please appear, please come back, my mother surely begged my father in her mind as two soldiers barged in, one tall, one squat.

As if he'd been summoned telekinetically, her husband materialized in the living room doorframe—his shirt retucked and his expression giving no hint at the panic he'd been on the verge of just moments before. His hands, which he'd soiled from digging in the dirt, were now as clean and unsuspicious as his expression. Papa had gotten the job done.

"We need five hundred zlotys and your jewels! Now!" the tall soldier demanded.

"Of course," Papa said, handing over a pile of cash, along with a charm necklace worth little and a man's pinky ring he had once found on a train without ever being able to identify the owner. He had left these two meaningless items in a side-table drawer before the soldiers arrived, anticipating they would want some jewelry.

"Surely you can't expect us to believe this is all you have," the soldier said as he gave his comrade a nod.

The short soldier quickly moved closer to Samuel and

my mother, and he pulled out his sidearm, waving it wildly in their direction. "I see you have so much that is valuable. I am sure you can do better." A dark expression crossed his face as he knelt down in front of Samuel—clearly taking notice of my brother's left hand.

Samuel's right hand clutched Mamishu's skirt, but his left hung at his side, closed in a tight fist.

"Why don't you open your hand, child?" the soldier asked in a gentle voice. "Let's see what you're hiding."

Mamishu was crying—terrified that the soldier had taken notice of Samuel. She knew her little collector wasn't hiding anything precious, though. In fact, she knew before he uncurled his doughy little fingers what would be resting on his palm.

"It's just a little rock, sir," Mamishu said. "He collects them."

Samuel revealed a small round gray stone—the kind of pebble you could find on any street in Poland. Samuel almost always had a rock in his hand or in his pocket—and he thought each one was unique and precious.

The soldier was not amused. He didn't like to be wrong—certainly not in front of Jews. He looked at my parents' faces. He looked at Grandma Dora. If any one of them had shown a hint of a smile, he would undoubtedly have shot them all.

No one was smiling.

"Please, help yourself to whatever the government may need," Papa interrupted.

By then, the first soldier was already searching through closets and drawers. He needed no invitation.

It seems so irrelevant now, but then it was heartbreaking for Mamishu to see her prized mink jacket pulled from the hall closet and slung over the soldier's arm. Papa had saved for a year to surprise her with this gift. She felt like one of those American movie stars from Hollywood whenever she wore it—even if it was just for a walk in the neighborhood.

A few long minutes later, as the soldiers gathered up their takings and prepared to leave, the shorter of the two spotted an ornate clock on twisted brass feet sitting on the edge of the hallway pedestal table. A gift her grandparents had given Grandma Dora on the day she became engaged, it had been handed down to Mamishu on her wedding day.

"Oh, shouldn't this be kept behind glass, something so special?" asked the squat soldier, gesturing toward the table. "You should be more careful with your keepsakes." Then he watched my mother to gauge her reaction as he used his hand to nudge the clock toward the edge of the table.

Mamishu held her expression steady. "Yes, thank you. I'll be more careful."

In slow motion, the diminutive man in uniform continued to guide the clock to the table's edge, waiting, waiting for a reaction.

When it was clear the fragile timepiece was about to fall, Mamishu gasped.

It was just enough to turn the soldier's blank expression into a nasty smile. "Oh!" he said as he gave the clock its final push. "My mistake."

The heavy heirloom fell to the floor with a crash. The glass face shattered into small pieces that flew to every corner of the hall. One twisted brass foot broke off. The clock was destroyed.

"You're so clumsy," the taller soldier said with a laugh, clapping his comrade on the back as they nodded toward Mamishu in false politeness.

And then they were gone.

When Mamishu closed the door behind them, Samuel folded his little body in half and, with his head bent to his knees, wailed with the weight of his whole being. He cried and cried and could not stop.

"No, Samuel, no." Mamishu rubbed his back. "It's all right. I'm not scared. Papa isn't scared. The men just needed some of our things to share with the new government. We are happy to help them."

Mamishu was trying hard to stay hopeful, but nights like this made it difficult. And deep in their gut all Jews in Żarki knew what they should expect. It had been laid out in perfect detail just a month earlier—on a day that came to be known as Bloody Monday.

2

BLOODY MONDAY

The war in Poland had begun on September 1, 1939, when German forces swept across the country in a *Blitzkrieg* (lightning war) attack. The next day, a Saturday, a German observation plane flew over Żarki at approximately one o'clock in the afternoon. Polish troops who had retreated from the German advance and sought refuge in our town spotted the aircraft and made a decision that would prove devastating. They fired shots from their rifles as the plane buzzed past. It was enough to gain the attention of the German military. By dinnertime, Żarki was under siege. German planes zipped across the sky, dropping bombs that ripped apart our homes. Each family wondered in the minutes of quiet between explosions if the next bomb would hit *their* house.

Two hundred and fifty-six Jewish homes burned down in my family's town that day, and in many cases, neighbors were trapped inside, hiding in cellars. The first bombs fell in a section of town called Leśniów. Next, it was our neighborhood. By all accounts, September 2 was a day of terror.

It probably sounds strange that Papa and Mamishu—and their entire community—didn't just pack suitcases instantly, throw on warm clothes, and trek into the woods until they reached a safer place. But home is home, and before the invasion Żarki had been a safe haven for Jews in Poland. In some Polish towns, Jews couldn't own land and businesses were highly restricted. In Żarki, though, where more than half the community was Jewish, life was better. Over three thousand Jews prayed daily at local synagogues, celebrated the Sabbath in their homes, and worked as craftsmen, merchants, and entrepreneurs who gained respect, even among some Catholic neighbors. There *were* some ugly examples of discrimination in Żarki. One market kept a sign in the window that read, "Don't buy from Jews! Support your own people." But Jewish-owned businesses still thrived in the town.

Żarki was not an easy place to leave, yet if anyone had guessed what was coming, there would have been no Jews remaining in Żarki after September 2, 1939. Everyone would have fled, attempting to escape the reach of the Nazis. As it was, though, most Jews of Żarki were hoping that when the bombing stopped and the German forces defeated the small Polish army and took charge, the invaders would peacefully reign over Poland, content to have won new territory for Hitler's empire.

When the sun came up Sunday, September 3, the day after the aerial attack, Mamishu, Papa, Samuel, and Grandma Dora all climbed up from the cellar. They couldn't believe the house was still standing. My mother assessed the living room with a mixture of relief and guilt. Some windows were cracked from the concussion of the bombs landing nearby, but the walls were all intact.

"*Baruch Hashem*," Bobeshi said aloud in Hebrew, praising God for their fortune.

Mamishu's face was wet with tears, though. "Those sounds—Israel, I can't get them out of my mind."

Papa didn't have to ask his wife which sounds. He also was haunted by the noises they'd heard in the darkness overnight—not just the explosions but also the voices of families shouting from inside homes that were burning to ashes. No one could save them. Everyone was tucked into cellars, praying for their own survival. The town was under siege. By daylight, Mamishu could see that the Jewish library in the distance had been badly damaged. Everyone in our community was proud of that place. A gift from a Zionist organization, it contained more than six thousand volumes and it served as sort of a cultural center in the Jewish quarter. Shelves were filled with literature from renowned poets and Jewish authors. Men gathered there twice a day to pray and to discuss the teachings of the Torah, the Jewish holy book.

Mamishu said she wanted to go check on her parents, Esther and Mordecai Jonisch, who lived nearby.

"Absolutely not," Papa insisted. He rarely argued with his wife, but now he was firm. "Sophie, do you understand what's happening? The bombing is only the beginning. This is war. The soldiers are coming."

My father was right. That Sunday, soldiers streamed into town from every direction. They arrived in cars, in trucks, and on motorcycles. Nazi troops marched through the streets dressed in black. We later learned they were part of the elite unit of the Nazi guard known as "storm troopers" and their objectives were to terrify and to destroy. Żarki was one of the first towns they invaded. Hours into that first day, it was clear that the Germans didn't plan to simply invade Poland; they intended to utterly dominate it.

Soldiers ripped machines out of factories, shattered glass

on storefronts, and shot up homes. They used dynamite to blow up a textile factory on the edge of town, preparing to steal the bricks that tumbled down from the chimney and load them onto a train to send to Germany. They even tore benches out of school classrooms. If they could have ripped clouds out of the sky, pulled apart the fluff, and scattered it over the streets, I think they would have done that, too. Both Jews and Polish gentiles watched helplessly as their property was destroyed. Jews, though, were especially targeted.

Another sleepless night passed, and on Monday morning every Jewish man in Żarki was ordered to the town center to report for labor shifts. Papa debated hiding in the cellar but then worried that his disappearance could put Mamishu and the family in even more danger. He assured Mamishu he would be fine, threw on a jacket, and rushed to join the others.

Papa wanted Mamishu to stay home while he was gone, but she did not listen. She respected Papa a great deal, but she knew her own mind and always followed it. Later that Monday, the second full day of the ground invasion, my mother left Samuel at home with Bobeshi and rushed silently toward her parents' house.

Leaving the gray limestone house on Sosnawa Street, she ducked onto a path nearby that would take her along a more inconspicuous route. She would have to pass the Jewish cemetery, but it would lead right to her parents' backyard. Very superstitious, Mamishu was always careful to walk along the perimeter of the cemetery and never, ever near the buried dead.

Was that crying?

Mamishu heard a desperate sort of sound that tugged at her insides. It was a child sobbing. Then came the sound of a man shouting. It sounded like he was speaking German.

Mamishu hid behind the wide trunk of an old birch tree and listened. The voices were coming from not far away. Mamishu knew she shouldn't look, but she did.

First, she saw a bright pink velvet dress and little black polka-dotted Mary Jane shoes strewn in the dirt. She squinted to see a little farther in the distance and recognized the face of three-year-old Sasha Beritzmann, who was standing next to a soldier.

The little girl was always at synagogue on Saturday mornings, dressed like a baby doll and sitting in her mother's lap. Whenever the congregants recited the Shema, a prayer that requires people to cover their eyes before God, Sasha giggled because she thought the women near her were playing peekaboo. She would laugh so hard that her mami sometimes carried her out of services.

In spite of having seen the dress on the ground, Mamishu was shocked to see the little girl naked. She heard more shouting from the German soldier. Sasha's parents were there, too. The soldier appeared to be ordering the parents to undress as well, because as he shouted in German, Mr. and Mrs. Beritzmann peeled off their clothes. Mrs. Beritzmann was trying to shield herself from the guard by turning her body away and covering herself with her hands.

The guard screamed again, this time in broken Polish that my mother could understand.

"Zakończeniu pracy!" Finish your work!

The uniformed soldier practically threw a large shovel at the stark-naked Mr. Beritzmann, who caught it in midair.

In his right hand, the soldier kept a pistol trained on Mr. Beritzmann's head. The terrified father began to deepen a hole in the ground that was quite large. They must have already been out here for a while.

Mamishu strained to see Sasha more clearly. The child was crying so hard that her face was red and swollen. Mrs. Beritzmann scooped her up and pressed the child's cheek against her own bare chest, trying to console her.

Mamishu wanted to run screaming at the group and rip

the gun out of the soldier's hand. She wanted to point it at *his* face instead. She wanted to give the Beritzmanns their clothes and their dignity back. But unarmed and helpless, she couldn't leave her hiding spot by the birch tree's wide trunk.

After a while, the soldier ordered Mr. Beritzmann to join his wife and daughter. The soldier waved his gun sideways, directing them to stand right in front of the freshly dug hole. He was deliberate about their placement. "Step to the right. Not so much. Step back!" he said in bad Polish.

The three did what they were told. Finally, the soldier commanded Mr. Beritzmann to hug his family. Mamishu watched with one eye, peering around the side of the birch. Mr. Beritzmann wrapped his bare arms around his wife and that baby girl she was holding so tight. Mrs. Beritzmann was sobbing and Sasha was screaming and Mr. Beritzmann was praying aloud, their naked flesh making them all the more vulnerable.

"Hush!" the soldier shouted at them. Then, softly, he repeated, "Hushhhhh. Hushhhh."

Mamishu couldn't see their faces because they were all looking down inside their close huddle, their heads pressed together tightly. They fell silent, though. Even Sasha. She had followed her mother's and her papa's lead and stopped crying, too.

Then *BAM! BAM! BAM!* The three shots were each perfectly placed. Naked and entwined together in an eternal embrace, the whole family fell backward into the big grave Mr. Beritzmann had just dug.

The soldier stood there with the strangest expression of satisfaction on his face. Mamishu could sense his deranged pleasure. She would never forget that man's expression as much as she wanted to rip the memory from her brain. It was as if the soldier yielded pleasure from death, like it was an art form to him.

When the soldier finally kicked some dirt into the hole and left the scene, my mother ran as fast as she could, on shaking legs, back to Sosnawa Street. She burst through the front door and fell onto the couch crying. Bobeshi and Samuel were both napping in their bedrooms, so for a long while she was alone with the evil of what she'd seen.

That evening at about six o'clock—around the time Mamishu was panicking that Papa wasn't yet home from his labor assignment with the German soldiers—there was a loud knocking at the front door. Before Mamishu could decide whether to hide or to answer it, her friend Malka came bursting through the door and into the living room.

Malka was frantic. "I don't know how the soldiers are getting these lists, but somehow they knew we had a teenage son in the house. Soldiers showed up this morning, waving their guns around and insisting that Avi report for duty. I said, 'He's only fourteen.' The soldiers didn't care. Avi left with Dan hours ago, and I got nervous, Sophie."

Malka drew a deep breath and then continued her story.

She had been waiting all day, but after no sign of her husband and son she walked to the square at the center of town and still couldn't find them. And then she saw the most horrific sight she had ever witnessed.

Mamishu braced herself. "Israel?" she asked in a muffled voice, her hand covering her mouth. "Is it my Israel?"

"No," Malka said quickly. "No, I didn't see him. He wasn't there." But then she continued, painting a vivid and torturous picture.

"A large group of gentiles had gathered near the square, and I slipped into the crowd. Nobody noticed me. I sidled my way toward the front and I saw . . ." Malka struggled to find the words. "I saw that the Kleins, the Adlers, and the Golds were forced to play some kind of game, I guess you could say. Their children, too—three whole families were lined up facing the brick wall that is standing where Mr. Mendel's shoe repair store caught fire. So what is that? Twelve, thirteen, fourteen people lined up with their noses practically pressed to the wall. Two soldiers had their guns pointed at the families, and one shouted, 'All right, my dirty Jew friends, let us find out who is strong among you. Everyone must keep their hands in the air and not move one muscle. If you lower an arm, we shoot you dead. Understand?'" Malka made her voice loud, mimicking the soldier's commands.

"Sophie, the crowd around me was laughing and applauding." Malka clapped her hands in an exaggerated fashion. "The other children, they are all at least twelve years old, but poor Hana Gold is—I mean *was*—only six. She started begging to lower her arms. 'Please, may I? It hurts,' she said. I could see her arm twitching. The crowd was still cheering around me, and then Hana's arm started to slip downward just a little bit. Before her little arm fell completely to her side, the soldier fired at the back of her head. Blood splattered everywhere and drenched the wall. Sweet Hana just collapsed like she was boneless."

Malka's tear-covered face was white as she recounted what she'd seen. "Oh, Sophie, Sarah Gold did what any of us would have done. She screamed and fell to Hana's side, kissing every inch of her face. Sarah's lips and cheeks were red with Hana's blood. I saw those two soldiers look at each other. Together I could hear them say, *'Eins, zwei, drei.'* They counted to three and pumped bullets into Sarah's body."

"Erik Gold?" Mamishu asked hesitantly. "Hana's father?"

"Erik—he didn't turn around or drop his arms, but I could see his whole body convulsing and—I don't know how to describe it—his cries were like no sound I've heard before. His back shook, his head bowed to his chest, but his arms stayed high in the air. I left. I ran out of there as fast as I could. I've still no idea where my Avi and Dan were taken!"

One hundred innocent people were killed in Żarki on the first full day after the Germans arrived. In Częstochowa, a city thirty kilometers to the north of Żarki, a notorious slaughter of one thousand Jews that day would cause September 4, 1939, to be remembered as Bloody Monday.

It was too late to leave Żarki. Anyone seen trying to flee the town was shot on the spot. As my father cleared debris from the streets as part of his assignment on Bloody Monday, he plotted an imaginary midnight trip outside the town through the thigh-high buckwheat fields and into the woods. But it was just too risky. My family had missed any chance to escape the war.

Over the next two weeks, restless panic affected the people of Żarki. Escape plans were made and then scrapped, because any plan was unworkable given the number of soldiers. Secret bunkers were built and doors were disguised.

Then came an announcement: "All Jewish men must report to the main synagogue for the night. Repeat, Jewish
men to the synagogue. Those who ignore orders will be arrested or shot on sight. All Jewish men—to the synagogue.
Sofort!" Right now!

Papa had been lost in silent prayer when the announcement came. He wasn't in synagogue, of course. He was
praying as he dug debris from a drainage trench for the
Germans.

What now? He wanted desperately to go home and see
Mamishu, Samuel, and his mother. He wanted to wash his
hands and eat a proper meal, rest his feet, and feel the safety
of his own home.

There was no choice, though. Nazi soldiers had shouted
their orders. Papa had to obey. It was early in the war, and
my father wasn't bold enough to test the system—yet.

3

THE ROUNDUP

My father closed his eyes for a moment as he entered the *shul*—the main synagogue in Żarki—on that September day. The *shul* was his second home: this house of prayer was where he started and ended every day, and where he studied the Torah.

He closed his eyes that evening because he knew that when he opened them he would see a painful scene. The temple had been desecrated. Artifacts had been ripped from the altar by the Nazi invaders. Pictures were torn down, benches were smashed in half, and walls were riddled with bullet holes.

Other Jewish men entered after my father, and then about a dozen German soldiers came in behind them, lugging bales of hay into the center of the room. Then they left the sanctuary and returned moments later, tossing rakes onto the floor.

"Time to make your beds, Jewish pigs," an officer said. "Tonight you sleep in the barn."

Papa raked hay into a corner of the room and made a cushioned area for himself, leaving space for Malka's husband and son, and for Mamishu's four brothers, Moniek, David, Sam, and Mullek, all of whom were just making their way over. His little group—so desperately tired that night—managed to find sleep quickly despite their beds of hay and the barrels of two guns trained on the crowd by German guards at the exit.

Back at home, a frightened Samuel crawled under the blankets next to Mamishu at bedtime and asked when Papa would be coming home.

"Soon," Mami lied. "Very soon."

Two days passed, and then the wives on our street finally decided they would search for their husbands. At sunrise, Mamishu and a handful of the other wives set off toward the synagogue, holding hands. Grandma Dora stayed back with Samuel, having promised Mamishu she would make sure Samuel remained safe.

On the street the wives passed soldiers, who fortunately just ignored them. When they arrived at the synagogue,

Mamishu peered in the window. Imagine her relief: Papa was there and very much alive. He looked weary. There were piles of flattened hay on the floor where the men had slept for two nights like a pack of stray dogs.

Mamishu tried to will Papa to look up and catch sight of her peering in the window, but Papa seemed lost in thought—or maybe in prayer. The men were all awaiting their work assignments for the day.

Mamishu knew that as the sun continued to rise more soldiers would begin stirring up trouble elsewhere in town. She raced back home, content to see that Papa was alive and looked physically unharmed.

That morning, Papa was ordered to a nearby field along with a large group of men. They were given shovels and told to dig a huge open pit. Then they were marched back to a place in town where horses lay dead from the aerial bomb attacks earlier that month. Perhaps the Germans had left the horses in place for so long just to defile the town further.

"*Mach schnell!*" the soldiers snarled at the group. Hurry up!

The rotting bodies of those dead horses had created a

stench so foul that even the Germans couldn't tolerate the nastiness of it. The men from the synagogue were told to grab the carcasses by their hooves and pull them to Koshigliver Street on the outskirts of town to be buried.

If the smell didn't make it hard to breathe, then the heavy labor did. Dragging those decaying nine-hundred-pound bodies was nearly impossible, even with ten laborers struggling together.

All day the men worked. At sundown, as they stood in the pit shoveling dirt onto the carcasses, Papa began wondering if he would ever be allowed to go home to sleep or eat. More than anything, he wanted to tell Mamishu that he was all right. He hadn't seen her peering in the window of the synagogue earlier, and he was desperate to reassure her.

Finally, a German officer named Schmitt shouted that they would be taking five men out of the trench. Papa looked up at the sky and prayed to the heavens he would be chosen.

Instead, the soldiers picked five workers my father knew well, including two teenage boys. One of them was Malka's son, Avi. Happy that Avi would be given a break, Papa allowed himself to feel jealous for only one moment before he returned to work.

But within moments, Papa was startled by an explosion of gunfire. He peered over the piles of dirt from the trench to see splatters of blood on a wall where those five men and boys had been standing. Now their bodies were crumpled on the ground. The workers hadn't been chosen for relief of duty; they had been lined up against the brick wall of a building near the field and murdered.

My father whispered a prayer under his breath: *"Sh'ma Yisrael Adonai Eloheinu Adonai Eḥad."* Hear, O Israel: the Lord is our God, the Lord is One.

Papa knew he would never tell Malka and Dan what he had witnessed. He would simply say, "Avi has gone to God." What crime had the boy committed? Had he worked too slowly?

Papa returned to his chore and dared not look up until Officer Schmitt finally shouted, "Run home, Jews!"

My father was well aware that the curfew imposed on Jews in town was fast approaching. He was relieved to hear one of his comrades ask the question he was thinking at that very moment.

"Sir—Officer Schmitt—doesn't our curfew begin in just a few minutes? If we are caught on the street after eight, we could be arrested or even killed."

Schmitt smiled as if he had just been delivered a

delightful gift. "Then I suppose you should be fast!" he shouted. "My Jew friend here is correct. Anyone found walking the streets in five minutes risks being shot on sight." The commander pulled out his pistol and aimed it at them.

With the barrel of a German Luger trained on their backs, Papa and the other men in his group sprinted home. It was like a physical-education class drill, except the teacher was an armed madman given the authority of an official lieutenant.

On this same day, Papa's friend Jacob Fischer had been ordered to the center of town for his work assignment. The bombings at the start of the month had left behind piles of rubble six feet deep. Jacob and others in his group were tasked with what had become a common job: clearing the mass of debris and sorting out reusable building material.

Two German soldiers were assigned to each Jewish man. The soldiers' only job was to stand directly by their laborer's side endlessly shouting, "Work faster, you lazy pig!" The soldiers would prick the points of their bayonets into the Jewish workman's sides as he heaved trash into wheelbarrows and wagons.

By twelve o'clock, Jacob was desperate for a lunch break.

Blood had stained through his shirt where a bayonet had caught him in the gut earlier. But at noon, there was no food and no rest for the laborers. Instead, the soldiers were replaced with a fresh contingent of guards who were full of energy and ready to imagine new kinds of cruelty.

These guards quickly took notice of Abe Turbetchsi, a visibly strong and broad Jewish man, and decided to have some "fun" with him.

The guards told Abe to put a large, heavy piece of equipment on his back that most men could scarcely lift alone, and run back and forth across the street. The quicker Abe ran, the more the soldiers whooped and yelled, "Faster, dirty Jew, faster!" as they ran alongside him, pricking Abe's flesh with their bayonets.

A group of people who had gathered to watch this scene began to laugh uproariously. Most Żarki gentiles were scared, victims of the invasion themselves. But a small band of hooligans took pleasure in laughing at a suffering Zyd (Jew). Perhaps in their own fear, they even wanted to appear to be siding with the invaders—to show eager cooperation.

These onlookers cheered and clapped when the German guards told Abe to sing a Polish folksong while he ran. Barely able to breathe, Abe chanted the song in a deathly rasp.

Finally, unable to take one more step, Abe faced his tormentors and screamed, "Kill me! Kill me now! Just kill me!"

The soldiers found this hilarious. The crowd's cheering grew louder.

But, to his tormentors, a bullet would have been all too humane for Abe at this moment. Instead, four soldiers used clubs to pummel him over the head, back, and legs until he collapsed. Then they raised their clubs at the rest of the Jewish laborers, and one soldier shouted, "Who's next?"

Jacob and his peers closed their gaping mouths and returned to work.

At the end of that violent day, Mamishu was waiting at home like every other terrified Jewish wife and mother in the town. Darkness was falling. The curfew was minutes away, and still no sign of Papa.

Little Samuel probably had not seen his mother move from the living room window all day. Bobeshi fed him and kept him entertained in the kitchen while Mamishu stood watch from sunup until, here it was, sundown.

Straining her eyes, she thought maybe she saw a figure rounding the corner onto their street. It was two men, actually, and they were running. Papa and my uncle Sam

Jonisch, whose house was not far away, were sprinting down the center of the road. Mamishu let out her breath, not realizing she had been holding it in. She opened the front door, and a minute later Papa was inside the living room, panting so heavily he sounded like a wild beast. His five-minute race to survival had left him speechless. Or maybe he just didn't want to speak.

Mamishu made him a nice, warm dinner of chicken soup with *lokshen* (noodles) and watched him stare at his bowl wordlessly for an hour, barely touching the meal.

He had always shared everything with his beloved wife, but on this night he sat silent.

So Mamishu shared something with him instead. "Israel," she said, touching her belly. "Darling, there is one good thing that is sure to come in the next year. There is one reason to just look ahead, my love."

Papa was so distracted by the terror of the day that he did not understand at first what she meant.

"We're going to have a baby, Israel. In the spring, Samuel will have a little brother or perhaps a little sister," she said proudly. She watched her husband's tired and drawn face turn pink with color.

If German guards had been blowing their whistles outside his door at that very moment, he still couldn't have stopped himself from smiling. He jumped to his feet and hugged my mother. And for the first time in three weeks he felt hope.

Mamishu held great hope, too. She had wanted another baby for a long time.

Now that she had told her husband, she was most anxious to tell her younger sister, Hilda Jonisch—her best friend in the world and her confidante from childhood.

Mamishu was one of seven siblings in a family in which everyone was close, but she and Hilda had a particularly special bond. They had shared a bedroom growing up in their loving but clamorous household and had also shared each other's secrets from the time they were small.

I'm having another baby! This spring, Hilda! Mamishu wanted to say, just imagining the look of delight on her sister's face, if only she could tell her the news.

But Hilda had taken a job in the Polish capital of Warsaw, 250 kilometers away. She had left many months before the invasion, and now it was impossible for her to return home. The movement of all Jews was completely restricted.

I suppose that's why the entire family was shocked about what happened seven months later on a spring evening in Żarki when a pickup truck made a surprising delivery.

4

WHAT SNUCK IN WITH THE LAUNDRY

By April 1940, the Germans had posted signs at the border of Żarki warning Jews not to leave. The punishment for leaving without permission was death. Other signs were posted on all roads coming into town, warning outsiders not to enter the ghetto—that is, the Jewish quarter.

But inside our little sealed-off world, life was returning to a strange version of normal. Żarki was considered an "open ghetto." In other words, it was not closed in by fences or barbed wire. There were simply checkpoints in the main section of town (which was primarily Jewish) and the warning signs aimed at anyone who dared sneak around those checkpoints. Life was as close to normal as any Jew in Poland could hope for during the war.

In between his long hours on work details, Papa made small repairs around the house, such as patching the windows, which had been cracked by the force of falling bombs. On Thursdays, Mamishu would pull Samuel in a wagon into the ghetto square, where food rations were distributed. She would get potatoes for soup, beets to make borscht, and sometimes a piece of meat to cook for Sabbath dinner. Mamishu walked slower those days, because I was growing like a lead anchor inside her.

On the walks back from the square, she would pass plots of barren land where homes had been destroyed in the bombings, but by now she no longer heard the ghosts of neighbors crying for help as she passed. This destruction just became background scenery in Żarki. Our town's landscape was now shaped like a broken heart; everyone stopped noticing so much.

My family could even honor the Sabbath again—privately, and in our own home. Papa would uncover the family treasures on Friday afternoons and fill the hidden kiddush cup with sweet red wine. He would lift the cup high in the air and welcome in the weekly Jewish holy day. Grandma Dora would light two candles, wave her hands toward herself three times to invite in the spiritual Sabbath queen, and cover her eyes as she recited the blessing.

Mamishu's sea-blue eyes would come to life again as she squeezed Samuel's hand and sang, *"A gute vokh! A mazldike vokh! Dos shtikele broyt kumt on mit mi. A gute vokh . . ."* A good week! A lucky week! The little piece of bread is earned with a lot of toil. A good week . . .

Mamishu loved to sing. She was quite dramatic and when she sang, she raised her eyebrows and exaggerated her hand movements like she was on a big stage. To others, Mamishu always seemed so pretty, even if she wasn't a natural beauty in the conventional sense. She carried extra weight and colored her cheeks with a bit too much rouge, but her translucent blue eyes and theatrical expressions drew people to her. In earlier years, my mother had even taken on roles at the local theater.

Those days were long past now. But there were still moments that called for celebration. One of those was coming up. The holiday of Pesach (Passover) would be observed, even in the ghetto.

Passover is a holiday that celebrates the ancient Jews' liberation from slavery. I know—you probably see the irony. The family was celebrating freedom at a time when Żarki's Jews were essentially German slaves. Still, Passover was too wonderful a holiday to neglect. It's jam-packed with lovingly preserved traditions, like dipping parsley into saltwater. The parsley marks spring and rebirth after slavery. The saltwater represents the tears of Jewish slaves.

That Passover of 1940, Mamishu's parents, Esther and Mordecai Jonisch, invited the entire family for the Passover feast. It would be an abbreviated meal. The holiday had to be condensed into the small window of time between the end of the workday and the start of curfew. It was Passover nonetheless, and everyone was excited.

"Sophie, that baby of yours must be about ready to join the world, wouldn't you say?" Grandma Esther beamed as she opened the front door with the smell of roasted chicken (an incredible treat) wafting out from behind her. "And, Dora, I'm so pleased you could join us," she added, motioning for my other grandmother to come inside. Esther Jonisch was dressed like she was going to the theater in the big city of Warsaw, even for this holiday meal inside a ghetto. She considered any event an occasion to wear taffeta, silk, and embroidered dresses that swirled around her ankles when she walked. No other woman in Żarki had a closet so impressive.

In appearance, Grandpa Mordecai was a simple man by comparison. He leaned down to kiss his pregnant daughter on the cheek as she entered. Then he scooped up Samuel. His long, dark beard tickled the side of Samuel's face. "Who is going to help me sing the Ma Nishtana tonight?" Grandpa Mordecai asked. The Ma Nishtana is a song with four questions that the youngest participant in any Passover feast is called upon to ask.

"Grandfather, you know I'm not the youngest anymore!" Samuel said, and giggled. "Baby Ruth will be here. It's her turn to sing!"

Ruth was the daughter of Mamishu's brother Sam and his wife, Cecia; she'd been born on August 1, 1939, exactly one month before the Germans invaded Poland.

"Well, that would be something!" Grandpa Mordecai said. "The song might sound more like this: 'Bla, la, la, dubby, dubby, wah, wuh, woo-woo.' How about you and Ruth sing together?"

Grandpa Mordecai was a deeply religious and serious sort of man, but he had a particular soft spot for his grandchildren.

More family arrived—Uncle David, Uncle Sam, Uncle Mullek, Uncle Moniek, their wives, and little baby Ruth—and soon the house was full of loud cheer.

Missing were Aunt Hilda, of course, and Mamishu's older sister, Ola, who years earlier had married a man named Aleksander Hafftka, moved to Warsaw, and had a baby named Sylvia. Ola and her family had fled Warsaw just before the Germans took control of the city. They ran to Wilno—a safe place for Jews at the time. Germans hadn't occupied Wilno yet, and my family assumed that Ola, Aleksander, and Sylvia were out of harm's way, but they all feared for Hilda. She was still living in Warsaw.

When everyone was seated, my father looked at Grandpa Mordecai and gave a nod that said, *Do you mind if I step in?* Grandfather acquiesced.

"Let's try to celebrate our being here together," Papa said, raising a glass of wine. "We understand how precious a gift that is." Papa looked down briefly, no doubt remembering those men whose blood had been spilled in the streets on Bloody Monday and in the weeks and months that had followed. He must have thought about Avi, about the Golds and the Kleins and the Adlers. The heavy pause carried great weight.

Then suddenly a loud thud at the front door broke that moment of reflection and frightened everyone at the table. At first, no one moved.

Bang! Bang! Bang!

Whoever was outside would not be ignored. The men at the table jumped up in unison to answer the door as Mamishu, Grandma Esther, and the others tucked all evidence of a Jewish celebration under the crocheted white tablecloth and in the drawer of the credenza.

This time, however, there was no reason for fear.

"What?"

"It can't be!"

"Where did you come from, you clever lady?"

The brothers were all talking and laughing at the front door.

My mother rushed from the dining room to the entryway and watched as Grandpa Mordecai looked up at the heavens and then pulled his youngest child in for a gigantic hug.

"It is like God answered me! You heard me, my God!" he exclaimed.

Aunt Hilda had returned.

Mami practically pried Grandpa Mordecai's arms off Hilda so that she could squeeze into the embrace.

Crying, Mamishu said, "Hilda! I didn't know when I would ever see you again!"

But Hilda pushed mother back gently so she could steal a look.

"Sophie, you have news for your little sister?" Hilda asked. Her chestnut-brown eyes must have sparkled with excitement. "Look how long you kept this secret from me!" she chortled. "You must be having a child *tomorrow*! A baby? Another baby!"

The laughing and the hugging could have gone on much longer if it weren't for Papa. He was always thinking two steps ahead. "Hilda, it is a miracle to see you here. But is it safe? How did you get home?"

"Hah! For that, you must all sit down," Aunt Hilda said

as she motioned the family back into the dining room. Papa dragged an extra chair from the parlor and squeezed it in at the table.

As they strolled to their seats, Mamishu and Hilda linked arms and tipped their heads together like two songbirds returning to their nest.

The family all leaned in, anxious to hear what Hilda would have to say. Maybe things were better in Warsaw. Maybe you could travel freely.

"I made a friend—a goy," Hilda said, using the Yiddish slang for someone who isn't Jewish. "His name is Gustaw and he's been very kind to me. I still work at the bank, you know. The Germans—they've allowed it. I pose no threat in my job there."

Hilda noticed that Grandpa Mordecai was already raising an eyebrow in disapproval. He wasn't very trusting of Poland's non-Jews, who had openly discriminated against his people for so many years. He was also very protective of Hilda, whose husband had left for America before the war—without Hilda.

"Oh, Father! Don't look at me that way. Gustaw is my friend," Hilda huffed. "I see him coming and going near the bank in the mornings, and he always waves hello—even though I'm a Jew."

Grandpa Mordecai continued to glare and Aunt Hilda continued to talk.

"Gustaw knew how much I missed my family, and he concocted a plan. He snuck me here in the back of his truck—all buried in dirty laundry like a regular stowaway. I held my nose for hours just to see you all!"

"You did *what?*" my father asked. "I know you've missed your family, but you could have been killed. You still could be killed for such an offense!"

Mamishu jumped in. "Hilda, you made it. That's all that matters. And you'll stay with us now. You'll be here in Żarki and we will take care of you."

My father and Hilda exchanged a knowing look.

"Sophie, darling," Hilda said, "I have to go back to Warsaw. If I don't, the Germans will soon learn I am missing. I could be jailed or deported for traveling without permission. You know I can't stay here. I just needed to see you all, to be home for Passover. But Gustaw is waiting for me. I'll return to Warsaw before morning."

Hilda couldn't help but ask her parents one question while she had everyone's attention. It was the question that had truly prompted her journey. She needed advice.

"Father, Gustaw believes he can get me to Wilno. Soldiers would never search for me there, and I could be with

Ola and Alexsander. They had talked of escaping overseas and they would take me with them. Father, I need your guidance. What should I do?"

"Absolutely not!" Grandpa Mordecai snapped. "Hilda! No more risks. No more daring escapes." He couldn't have been as confident in what he would say next. "Hilda, this situation in Poland can't last. You need to stay in Warsaw until the war ends, my sweet daughter. The conflict will be over soon enough."

Hilda probably knew what his answer would be before she asked him. Of course he would choose caution. This was her beloved father, though. Hilda felt she must follow his advice.

I wish I could explain now how life-changing that one decision would be for my aunt Hilda. But no one could have guessed it that night.

Hilda paused for a beat and then reached for the glass chalice of wine in front of Mamishu's plate. "Well, then." Hilda forced herself to stay positive. It was one precious evening with her family, and she wouldn't squander it. "Let us celebrate Pesach and toast to my nephew or my niece soon to join big brother Samuel!" Just then Hilda noticed the look of confusion on Samuel's face and she leaned over the table to touch his cheek. "I think you've forgotten your aunt, haven't you, my love? I'm your auntie Hilda." It hurt

Hilda's heart to realize she had been away so long that her own nephew did not recognize her.

But there wasn't time for disappointment. The Passover seder was waiting. Prayers were chanted, pickled herring and potato pudding were devoured, and long embraces were held.

By morning, Hilda was gone.

Ten days later, Mamishu went into labor and I was born on May 2, 1940. I shared all of my mother's fair features, with milk-white skin, a mess of dirty-blond curls, and bright blue eyes—rare coloring for a Jew. They named me Michael. In Hebrew the name means "Who is like God?" Papa said it was the perfect name for a little boy whose arrival brought overwhelming joy where there should have been no happiness. Even as German soldiers patrolled the streets of Żarki outside, my parents welcomed me into a Jewish home in the most traditional way. Eight days after my birth, they held a *bris*, a ceremony that begins with the blessing *Baruch Ha-Ba* (Blessed is the one who has arrived). Neighbors and friends gathered in the Bornstein family living room to witness my circumcision, a procedure that solidified my Jewish status.

By May 1940, scores of Jews in Poland had been moved

to work camps or to closed ghettos with walls and barbed-wire fencing around them—like prisons. In the city of Łódź, more than two hundred thousand Jews were officially sealed in to a small section of town on the first day of May. Germans renamed the city Litzmannstadt (Litzmann's City) to honor a fallen World War I general.

In contrast, Żarki still felt like home to its Jewish population, even if home was never quite the same. In the open ghetto, everyone stayed in their own houses as long as they followed the rules of the Nazi invaders. My parents felt blessed for this small grace.

We didn't know what was coming. Outside the borders of Żarki, more changes were in the works. Nazi ruler Adolf Hitler and his henchmen were perfecting their plan to eliminate Jews from the face of Europe. It would eventually be called the Final Solution.

The wheels of evil were rolling smoothly now. We didn't even hear them coming.

5

THE JUDENRAT

It was March 1941. Nearly a year had passed since I had been born, and despite my parents' continued optimism, conditions were getting worse, not better. Food rations were shrinking. Instead of two loaves of bread per week, my family made do with just one. Instead of one full sack of hearty potatoes, Mamishu returned from the square with only a handful of soft, blemished ones each week.

With hunger came illness. There was never enough medicine to go around, and when an illness hit one household, it often spread to many. There was no letup in the long, grueling work assignments for men and teenage boys. The most pressing job was keeping the main road in good repair and clear of debris or snow. It served as an important thoroughfare for German soldiers traveling across Poland.

Still, Żarki remained an open ghetto and, for that, families were thankful. Everyone returned to his own home each night. And now Papa had an important role inside our community. Right after I was born, the Nazi government declared that every ghetto and town in Poland must have a Judenrat—a formal council of Jewish leaders. The Nazi regime declared that these leaders would help the German army enforce rules and maintain order among Jews. Membership on the Judenrat was not necessarily a coveted role. Jews quickly came to view Judenrat leaders as traitors, assisting the enemy. Papa wasn't given a choice, though. The elders in his own Jewish community selected him to be president of Żarki's Judenrat.

He hated that title—president—and he loved it at the same time. He dreaded the looks from neighbors who viewed him as one step removed from the Nazi enemy. He also prayed that his role could help him save the family.

"Why worry so much, Israel?" Mamishu would ask. "You don't have a choice. You fret so much about things you can't control."

It was true. Papa simply had to do his best to protect those he could. He had a plan, too. Maybe it was too radical, too risky. He had to try to make the most of his position, though.

"Sophie, do you think money can talk louder than weapons?" Papa asked her one night.

It was a weekday evening and Mamishu was in the

kitchen boiling red berries in a pan over the stovetop to make compote. She may not have known exactly what he meant, but she probably had a feeling about where this conversation was headed.

"I think you need to follow the Germans' orders, stay quiet, and stop plotting," she told him. "Stop thinking so much, Israel. You should have realized by now that our best hope is that the war ends. It's only a matter of time."

Papa said nothing. And since he didn't protest, Mamishu continued. She had been at her mother's house that morning and had seen a copy of an underground newspaper—a newspaper that was being printed and distributed secretly among Jews in the region.

"Israel, did you see the newspaper? It says Britain is pressuring the United States to join the Allied forces who are fighting the Nazis. If America joins the British, the German army will crumble. It's going to happen, and if—"

"Just hear me out, Sophie," Papa said, cutting her off gently. "I was thinking . . . there's still so much wealth here in Żarki. The Zimleichs have thousands of zlotys hidden underground, just like us. So do the Birnbaums and the Heitels. If I can gather enough funds, perhaps I can persuade some soldiers to loosen the rules a little around here. The German guards don't speak Yiddish, but the language of money must be universal."

"Israel, please," Mama implored. She reminded him about what had happened to their friend Avrom Frish.

Avrom had tried to reason with the soldiers that he needed to be placed on another work assignment because his right shoulder was too weak for bricklaying. Instead, he was taken to the cemetery the next morning and made to dig his own grave. "Two guards shot him right there on the spot! And then they were too lazy to drag his body the extra five feet into the hole. They left him right where he fell. These are the animals you're going to start business with, Israel?"

"Sophie, I know you don't want to accept it any more than I do, but conditions have been worsening. Jews can't do business by the light of day. The men in town—we work for free for the Germans from sunup to sundown. We're running out of money! We're running out of food! And I'm hearing stories, Sophie. Terrible stories about Jews imprisoned behind barbed wire and—"

"Stop!" Mamishu said, raising her voice. She motioned to Samuel—who was showing me how to build a pyramid with pots from the kitchen while Grandma Dora sat nearby. "You have two children, Israel. I know you think you can make things better—but you could also make them much worse. When Jews fight the system, it's not a pretty sight, and you're—"

Papa stopped her there. "*You're* a pretty sight, Soph." He planted a big kiss on Mamishu's bright red lips. He was trying to change the subject. No doubt my father was already sorry he had asked Mamishu for counsel. He really just wanted someone to tell him he was right. Frankly, his mind was already made up.

He told Mamishu he would discuss it with her brother Mullek at Shabbat dinner instead. Mullek would see his point.

In the meantime, Papa bent down to ruffle Samuel's hair and lift me up in his own strong, safe grip.

"Would I do anything to put my *liblings*—my loved ones—at risk?" he asked, and smiled at Mamishu.

Mamishu tried not to smile back. She was worried.

"Mullek will like my plan," Papa said. "It's worth a try."

6

LOOK FORWARD

There weren't many opportunities for the whole extended family to get together in the ghetto. Twelve-hour work shifts for the men and dwindling resources at the market square made gatherings difficult. The Germans, always fearful of a Jewish uprising, didn't allow large groups of Jews to publicly gather at the synagogue, so there was no group prayer at *shul* anymore either. When the Bornstein and Jonisch families did gather, it was cause for celebration.

Days after Mamishu warned Papa against negotiating with Nazi soldiers, my father was still working on his plan. He looked forward to hosting a Sabbath dinner, and that week he had more than prayers on his mind.

It was incredible what the family managed to do, even within the constraints of the ghetto and with tapering rations. Grandma Esther brought baby greens and herbs that had miraculously sprouted early in her backyard more than a month before the growing season. Grandpa Mordecai had tucked away bottles of kosher wine he saved for just these occasions. Uncle Mullek had traded a link of a gold watch chain he kept hidden for a large chicken at the market, and Mamishu had kneaded and twisted a little dough into sweet challah for a special Shabbat. Inside my home, everything smelled and tasted as it should—if even just for the evening.

"Do you want to help, *zeisele*—sweetheart?" Grandma Esther's knees creaked as she bent to lift me off the ground and onto her hip.

She handed me a ladle, but instead of stirring the soup I used the big spoon to slap at the bubbling broth and watch it splash against the interior of the pot. Ever patient, my grandmother put her free hand on top of mine, and slowly, slowly we stirred the pot together.

Here we were, in a home filled with as much love as angst, welcoming the Sabbath in a world that held untold dangers just outside our doors. Everyone tried hard on those nights to only look forward. "Next year—in a free Poland!" Papa raised our kiddush cup and toasted to the future. We were sitting two to a chair at the dining room table. Our family was laughably large. Mamishu's brothers were all there, along with their wives, Bobeshi, and of course Samuel and me.

When the last of the homemade delicacies had been devoured and Samuel and I fell asleep to the melody of our relatives' voices outside our bedroom door, Papa motioned to Uncle Mullek to join him on the back porch.

Mamishu scrambled to the kitchen, where she pretended to be mopping down the counters with a wet rag. There, she could watch the shadow of these two men, her brother and her husband, through the kitchen window. The slow nods, the handshake at the end of their conversation, a hug between two men who rarely showed this kind of affection—it only served to make her more nervous. "No, Israel. No," she said out loud inside the empty kitchen.

At least she thought she was alone. Mamishu hadn't noticed that Grandma Esther had slipped into the kitchen, too, and was now standing quietly beside her.

"Always look forward," her mother said, kissing Mamishu on the cheek. The two women stood there in the kitchen for a long time, holding hands and watching the shadows of men outside who would be helping determine the fate of Żarki.

The next day, Papa called a special meeting of the Judenrat. The men met behind closed doors at the old library, which still bore the scars of those first days of the war. Inside, though, the community had worked hard in off-hours to nail shelves back onto the walls and return treasured books to their rightful spaces. The library was officially kept locked and shut in an effort to protect its contents from Nazi soldiers or vandals, but secret meetings were often held inside.

Papa laid out the plan to his trusted council members, and all agreed to put it into effect immediately. There was a sixty-minute window to get things done each day. Jewish men returned home from work assignments at about seven o'clock, and curfew started at eight. In that small window of time, Judenrat members knocked on doors, collecting contributions of their own. This time, donations were voluntary.

The men collected from the wealthiest Jews in town first, then fanned out across the Jewish quarter, taking smaller contributions from other families. Some people were skeptical to begin with—distrustful of anyone asking for money, even their own community leaders. Judenrat members in some towns would notoriously use their positions to try to benefit themselves. In this atmosphere of desperation it was hard to know whom to trust.

"Please, I heard footsteps inside and I know someone is home," Papa would say gently as he stood outside people's doors. "I promise, no one is in trouble."

The Judenrat was responsible for choosing people to be sent outside town for long-term labor assignments. My father had to enforce Nazi demands for contributions. He had to announce new German restrictions on Jews and was obliged to turn in those who disobeyed. It was easy to understand why some people might have feared my father. Judenrat members could easily be viewed as the enemy, no matter how benevolent they tried to be.

Efraim Monat, Papa's second-in-command, pleaded with his neighbors: "Just hear me out. This money could make life bearable. Conditions could change. Is that money doing you so much good now—buried underground? You've got to give us a chance."

In two and a half weeks of knocking on doors, not one family turned the Judenrat away without making at least some donation to the new fund. An enormous secret pot of money was collected, and Papa felt sure that fund was going to improve all of their lives. Maybe it could even save their lives. First, though, he had to face the most terrifying man in Żarki.

Do you remember how cool and calm Papa appeared to be when the German army stormed into the family's house for contributions? My father had an uncanny ability to hide his fear, according to my mother. Often, even she didn't know when her husband was nervous about something.

The meeting he was waiting to have, however, would require superhuman bravado.

Papa would have to find just the right moment. In the meantime, the men of Żarki reported for duty each day to the guards in charge. In winter, they shoveled snow for hours to keep the heavily traveled main roadway clear. In spring and summer, they filled holes in the pavement and kept debris off the path.

Once, they had orders to build a large, modern bathhouse in town. Dozens of Jewish men worked tirelessly to build it by hand over many months. But when the work was done, no Jews were permitted to use it.

Some Jewish men were drafted to help with engineering work on the nearby Leśniowska River. Some were sent outside town to the larger city of Częstochowa to work on an irrigation project.

Papa and other members of the Judenrat were mostly spared hard physical labor. But one of the worst assignments was reserved for them: collecting the bodies of murdered friends and neighbors. Jews caught illegally escaping the checkpoints around Żarki were shot on sight. Soldiers then contacted the Judenrat to retrieve the bodies, wherever they fell. Often, by the time Papa got to the bodies, any-thing valuable—even gold teeth—had already been stolen from the corpses.

No one complained to the Germans. Complaining got you killed. The laborers also learned to work fast. Working slow got you killed. They were released from work at seven and were sealed in their houses by eight o'clock in the eve-ning. Stepping outside after curfew would get you killed.

Papa and Mamishu always clung to signs of hope and remained ever grateful that at the end of each night we all went to sleep under one roof, together as a family. At the end of a difficult day, Papa would look at us and say, *"Gam ze ya'avor."* This too shall pass. This was the motto Mami-shu and Papa always professed. According to Jewish legend, if you say it enough times, it will make an unhappy man blissful.

"Soph! Mama! Listen to this!" Papa came in the house shouting to my mother and grandmother one day in late June 1941. He had received a copy of an underground news-paper. The edition was short. All of them were short, actu-ally, so that the people risking their lives to distribute the papers could hide them easily in their sleeves and pant legs.

Papa's eyes darted back and forth across the front page.

The newspaper had a report quoting the president of the United States, Franklin Delano Roosevelt, who had given a radio address only weeks earlier, on May 27. Papa read in his best presidential voice: "We do not accept, we will not permit, this Nazi 'shape of things to come.' It will never be forced upon us . . ."

My father was beaming. "The president of the United States, Sophie! He's made an emergency declaration and is readying the U.S. military. He's not declaring war, but his words—it sounds like America could be planning to join the Allied forces soon. Listen!" He scanned the report and then read: "If we believe in the independence and the integrity of the Americas, we must be willing to fight . . ." He skipped ahead. "We will not accept a Hitler-dominated world . . . We will accept only a world consecrated to freedom of speech and expression—freedom of every person to worship God in his own way—freedom from want—and freedom from terror."

Papa slapped the paper onto the table. "It's not a declaration of war, Soph, but he's sending a message and it is grand!" Roosevelt's words sounded so far from the life they knew right then, his message rang like poetry in their ears. "Freedom of every person to worship God in his own way . . . freedom from terror." If America valued and protected such things, then it sounded like heaven.

"This is it, Israel! The United States knows it must join the war effort!" My mother and grandmother had been listening to Samuel practice reading before Papa walked in the door. Mamishu took my brother's studies quite seriously, but now she tossed his book in the air and grabbed Samuel's two hands—pulling him onto his feet.

"The war will soon be done and gone. Żarki will see a brand-new dawn. The Germans will have to say they're wrong, and la, la, la, la, la, lala . . ." Mamishu could make a song out of anything, and right now she felt like singing!

Papa lifted me and spun me around, always quick to get caught up in Mamishu's theatrical enthusiasm, while Bobeshi clucked her tongue at us and pretended to be annoyed with all the fuss.

Even amid the quiet sorrow of the Żarki ghetto my mother could find a way to keep things light. She still spent time each morning brightening her cheeks and her lips with rouge and red lipstick—careful, though, to be sparing with the last of her reserves.

Unlike my parents, a majority of Jews in Żarki were religious conservatives. Many of the women dressed in long, simple dark clothing and kept their heads covered. The men dressed in black coats and hats and wore *payot*—side curls of hair over their ears in traditional Orthodox Jewish style.

Mamishu and Papa were part of a progressive movement in town that, before the invasion, had been growing. Religion and tradition were very important to them, but they wore it inside their hearts more than they wore it in their outward attire. Papa dressed in modern suits and shirts and favored city trends over old-fashioned Jewish dress.

Mamishu loved to style her blond hair with a side part, and she dressed in bright florals of blue and coral. Somewhere in every ensemble, she wore a splash of yellow—whether it was a brass broach or a sun-colored flower pinned in her hair. Maybe it was silly to care about appearances or hang on to any sense of vanity in the ghetto, but Mamishu always said that trying to make herself pretty was a way for her to feel human.

One thing you could count on inside Nazi-occupied Poland, though, was that whenever hope appeared it was always closely followed by torment. Days after that impromptu dance in our living room, more trouble arrived. There was suddenly no amount of citrine-colored fabric or rose lipstick that could hide the darkness outside our doors.

The Germans had armed a group of Polish guards and

put them on a team assigned to Żarki. This was a particularly brutal group. We had always been nervous when we left our homes, but suddenly it became impossible to even cross the street without being harassed or even attacked by the guards. They took pleasure in spilling Jewish blood. To call them bullies—well, that would have been a grand understatement.

Mamishu wouldn't leave the house the week the new team of guards arrived. We had just a handful of potatoes remaining in the cupboard, a little cream, and stale bread.

Walking to the town square was out of the question. The Polish guards beat every person they caught traveling the streets, no matter what time of day. Papa himself came home one night limping horribly after a guard had slammed a club against the back of his knee. Uncle Moniek's nose was broken when a guard jumped out from behind a tree, roaring like a wild animal as he came at my uncle with a baton. Then he punched Uncle Moniek square in the face, leaving him bloodied and bruised. They were bullying bandits, not law enforcement.

By Friday of that week, life in the ghetto was simply unbearable. The time had come to dig into the Judenrat fund and have that meeting for which my father had been waiting.

7

MONEY TALKS

Every Monday, Papa met early in the morning with Officer Schmitt, the head of the local Gestapo—the Nazi police— in the region. Not long after Papa was named Judenrat president, Officer Schmitt had assigned Papa to the role of Judenrat police chief as well. This was a role my father especially feared holding. What if he was ordered to kill a fellow Jew? What if he was forced to impose brutal restrictions or jail innocent neighbors? It was the reason a lot of Żarki residents were distrustful of my father. He had a reputation for being kind, but when you give a man power and a title, it could change him. Jews had, after all, witnessed what effect that had had on the band of Polish guards.

The Monday after the guards arrived in the ghetto, Papa stuffed his pants pocket with Polish banknotes. He and other Judenrat members had collected more than two thousand zlotys at a time when money was immeasurably scarce. That would be the equivalent of about five hundred dollars today. Papa knew the time had come to use the first batch of collected money.

My father gathered his courage as he approached the town's former bootmaking shop, which the Gestapo had taken over and was now using as a base. He knew that Officer Schmitt was likely to be alone, since his soldiers always walked the streets at that hour, looking for suspicious activity as the sun came up over Żarki. Aside from the patrols, the town was mostly quiet.

Fear had heightened my father's senses so that the smell of leather buried deep in the walls was almost overpowering as he entered the room. The shuffle of his own feet had never sounded louder, and he could feel his heart racing as he stepped in front of the Gestapo leader.

"Officer Schmitt," Papa said in his developing German tongue. "I'd like to speak with you about the new guards." *Creak.* His shoes made noise as he shifted weight. "They are making it more difficult for me to maintain my own people's trust. The guards—they are ruthlessly beating Jews in the ghetto. There does not seem to be reason behind their attacks. They are simply attacking at random, without provocation or cause."

Officer Schmitt was quiet a moment. Papa could hear only his breathing.

Then he stood up and walked over to my father. "Surely, Bornstein, you aren't intending to *complain*. You should be lying down at my feet and thanking me, your town has it so good. Jews across this country are sleeping behind barbed-wire fencing and iron bars. You go home to your soft pillows and wool quilts each night. I'll tell you what becomes of complainers. Last month—"

"Officer Schmitt," Papa interrupted. "I wondered simply if *anything* might inspire you to reassign the Polish guards somewhere outside Żarki. My community is willing to do anything at all to see that *your* needs are met. Please, Officer Schmitt, give it some thought."

Glaring at my father, Schmitt pulled his Luger from its holster and then pressed the tip of his pistol into Papa's forehead. With the barrel against his skull, Papa had never before had his ability to stay calm tested so dramatically. And yet he didn't flinch as Schmitt—with the smell of Sobieska vodka wafting off his lips—whispered, "You will not ever interrupt me again. I am an officer of the Third Reich, you dirty Jew!"

"Of course," Papa said. "I intend no disrespect, Officer Schmitt. I only wanted to provide you with assistance *however* you may require it."

The meaning for Papa's emphasis on the word "however" finally resonated with Schmitt. Papa watched as the switch seemed to click in the officer's malevolent mind. When a few moments had passed and Schmitt still had not pulled the trigger, Papa wordlessly reached into his pocket and pulled out the banknotes.

It was so bold a move—bribing an officer of the German police!—that Schmitt almost laughed. He had to admit, he said, that Israel Bornstein had guts. Schmitt probably could have used that extra cash, too. Wartime had put a strain on every family, even in Germany.

"Why don't I just take this cash and replace it with a bullet in your brain?" Schmitt asked, his dark eyes blazing.

Papa had no choice but to be direct. "I believe there is more where this came from, Officer Schmitt. But I'm afraid I'm the only person who can collect such discreet funds from the community. A bullet won't find you more buried treasure."

Within twenty-four hours of that conversation, the band of barbarous guards in Żarki was reassigned to a neighboring town. They never returned.

When a thirteen-year-old boy was arrested for missing a day of work in Żarki and his sentence was death, the jailhouse doors suddenly opened after Papa appeared with a large satchel at the front of the prison.

My father used the Judenrat fund to obtain two hundred legal travel visas for families desperate to escape Żarki. Many of those families made it all the way outside the borders of Poland to find safety and refuge. Hundreds more were able to escape through the woods at night or hide in bunkers with money from the Judenrat to sustain them. Papa's plan was working.

And so it went for about a year. Kosher butchers were forbidden from properly preparing meat for Jewish meals in Poland, but in Żarki, the kosher butcher's life was spared because of the Judenrat's deliberately spent funds. The last of the open ghettos in Poland were being shut down and inhabitants deported to camps, but Jews in Żarki slept in their own beds, with their families, inside a world protected by money—and by at least one very greedy German police officer.

8

PREDICTIONS FROM THE UNDERGROUND

For many months, the Judenrat's system of bribery was quietly effective, allowing Jewish citizens of Żarki to survive day-to-day life. Conditions were deteriorating, though.

Refugees from other ghettos were being pushed into the town. Earlier that year, 250 refugees from Plock, a town about three hundred kilometers to the north, were relocated to Żarki, and most households took in at least one family. We, too, had visitors for a long time until the family who stayed with us was moved again for a work assignment in Częstochowa. More people meant shrinking rations. Food was scarce. Funds were scarce. It was certainly true in the ghetto, and it was even true for gentiles outside our quarter. There simply wasn't enough to go around.

Papa wrote to the American Jewish Joint Distribution Committee (JDC). The aid group was authorized to operate out of Warsaw, helping send food and medicine to communities that faced the greatest need. With help from the JDC, the Judenrat set up a soup kitchen that could feed hundreds of people at a time.

But when the soup kitchen first opened, not one person showed up to get a meal. The problem, it seemed, was that Jews in Żarki were too proud to take handouts. So the Judenrat adjusted its approach, working instead to deliver meals to the very doors of the most needy in town, quietly and without judgment.

Before long, though, those discreet deliveries would not be necessary. Within weeks of the soup kitchen's opening, the food situation grew even more dire. Everyone was running out of supplies. Few Jews could pretend they had enough to survive, and eventually the soup kitchen was sustaining almost the entire community.

In mid-1941, there was also an outbreak of typhus in our area of Poland. It was the second time the potentially deadly disease had spread through the region since the war began. Typhus is a horribly contagious virus transmitted by lice. It causes high fevers, aches, rashes, and vomiting—and in our depressed community with little means or medication, typhus spread wildly with deadly results.

One day, Mamishu wondered why I hadn't woken up. I

was always an early riser; by the time Mamishu's eyes opened most mornings, I was already flipping through picture books on the end of her bed, pointing at images and pretending to read.

But on this morning I was still fast asleep. She knew before she touched my head with her lips that I would be hot as fire. When she put cold, wet rags on my forehead and legs, I startled and woke up. She lifted my shirt to do the same and found a light pink rash up and down my torso.

Over the next week, Mamishu worked hard to make sure I drank enough water and ate a little something every day. She would dip my legs in a bucketful of cold water, and she got me medicine prescribed by a doctor.

Even after the fever broke, I would wake in the middle of the night with a deep, barking cough that hurt my chest. My frightened parents took turns calming me back to sleep.

The cough lasted for weeks, and Mamishu was vigilant about keeping Samuel, her "big boy," away from me, so that he and the rest of the family would stay safe. Miraculously, Samuel never caught typhus and I showed my first signs of being an innate survivor. I beat the illness and was as healthy as any toddler once the cough finally cleared.

Papa, Efraim Monat, and Lejzer Steinem—the top three

Judenrat officials in Żarki—had created an infirmary in the ghetto, and its two doctors had to do more than just treat patients. Some local gentiles who already carried deep-seated resentment toward Jews were convinced we were to blame for the typhus outbreak.

"You need to exterminate the Jewish vermin in the ghetto, or lock them inside!" our countrymen said, appealing to the German soldiers. "They are to blame for this illness that is plaguing all of us. Cut it off at the source!"

As the Germans contemplated a decision, the Judenrat once again intervened. With help from the two doctors who treated every Jewish patient in Żarki, including one professional named Dr. Margalit, the Judenrat provided medical evidence that showed the disease originated outside the ghetto. Judenrat funds again protected all of us.

The money also allowed some former business owners to quietly engage in commerce within Żarki, and even outside city limits on occasion. Some Jewish businessmen were allowed to travel to other towns for trade as long as they quickly returned. Minor violations of Gestapo rules, like breaking a curfew, suddenly didn't seem so offensive when a wad of banknotes appeared.

Sometimes Papa used his influence to get permission to travel to larger cities where food wasn't quite so scarce. He would pay three hundred zlotys for fifteen pounds of flour, then bring it back to parcel out among households or have Mamishu, Bobeshi, Grandma Esther, and their friends bake bread for the neighborhood.

Samuel even went to "school" some days. My cousin Ruth's uncle, a very generous and well-respected businessman in town named Moshe Zborowski, used his own hidden stash to pay teachers who secretly educated children in the ghetto, now that formal schools were shut down for all Jews. Moshe was my aunt Cecia's brother-in-law and his many kindnesses were well-known in the town.

In 1940, the Japanese government signed an alliance with Germany, and on December 7, 1941, it shocked the United States with a surprise attack on the U.S. naval base at Pearl Harbor in Hawaii. The next day, the United States declared war on Japan, and within a few days was at war with Germany, too. My parents had been so eager for America to join the Allied forces against Hitler, but when it finally happened it brought little change. Still, the situation had at least plateaued in Żarki.

In my household, Papa rushed home before curfew each night and we would eat dinner as a family in the dining room. Meals were almost always the same: potato soup for breakfast, lunch, and dinner and sometimes fresh-baked bread to dip in the broth.

But as Polish Jews under Nazi rule learned time and again, just when they began to feel complacent, their world would be turned upside down. In the summer of 1942, no bribe was big enough to stop what was coming. Żarki began operating just like a closed ghetto. There was still no fencing, but it became impossible for Papa to leave town. The curfew was enforced with no exceptions; soldiers let no misstep slide.

And then came the rumors that the ghetto would soon be liquidated, emptied out. On September 22, trains began deporting people from the nearby Częstochowa ghetto to Treblinka, the forced labor and extermination camp in eastern Poland opened by the Germans in July 1942. Everyone guessed Żarki would be next.

Over the next two weeks, there were more attempted escapes from Żarki than there had been in three years of war. People fled through the woods at night. Some were caught and murdered, but many ran free.

Efraim Monat, the high-level member of the Judenrat, used connections he had with German headquarters in the district. He won legal travel permits for hundreds of families desperate to flee before the deportations. Many more families ran at night to the attics of some kindly Christian neighbors who would risk their own lives to hide them. The ghetto, once overcrowded with Jews, was hollowing out. Few people could ignore the gruesome rumors and the reports from underground newspapers.

Frightening articles claimed that throughout Poland thousands of Jews at a time were being rounded up and deported for what the Germans called "resettlement to the east." The men, women, and children were packed onto freight trains and taken to concentration camps where their suitcases and the last of their belongings were abandoned at the gates. None of those "resettled" ever returned. Witnesses were quoted in articles as saying that outside the camps, the smell of burning flesh choked the air from morning until night.

Honestly, it was too much to comprehend. What evil could prompt a government to destroy masses of innocent humans—if that's what was happening? Many people in Żarki refused to believe that such death camps were in operation. Papa and Mamishu were terrified at the news, but they, too, felt the reports must have been exaggerated.

Papa knew that if deportations to prison camps of any sort were happening in towns farther west in Poland, there was little chance the Judenrat could stop them in Żarki. He also knew that if his town was targeted for deportations, he would be making many of the decisions about who boarded the trains and who stayed behind. The title of Judenrat president felt like a sixty-pound chain wrapped around his neck, strangling him with the weighty horror of each decision to come.

On October 6, 1942, Papa woke up early. He would head to the library that morning for a special meeting of the Judenrat. He knew a deportation was imminent—maybe it would even happen later that week.

"Gam ze ya'avor," Papa whispered softly to us all. This too shall pass. He and Mamishu exchanged a heartbreaking nod over a breakfast of stale bread crusts and water. He wiped a few crumbs from his lips with the back of his hand and then got up from his chair. He kissed each of us like he always did when he left the house, put on his hat, and started walking to the Jewish library for his meeting.

Staring out the front window, Mamishu could do nothing but watch him walk away.

Before Papa had even crossed the street, though, Officer Schmitt—the cruel Gestapo leader my father knew so well—approached him briskly for a conversation. Schmitt, at six foot four, was such a broad, imposing man that it must have looked like he was bending down to scold a child when he addressed my father.

The soldier simply whispered something into Papa's ear and walked away robotically.

Mamishu said that all color drained from my father's face and he did something she had never seen him do before. He let out a loud, primal, thunderous shout she could hear through the windowpanes—and he broke down in tears.

9

COUSIN RUTH

Terrifying, uncertain decisions had to be made across Żarki as the situation worsened. Was it safer to stay at home and cooperate with the Nazis, to flee through the woods at night, or to seek a secret hiding place right there in the community? My family made our choice; my cousin Ruth's family made a very different one. Born one month before the German invasion, my cousin remained an only child as the war dragged on. Her parents, my uncle Sam and aunt Cecia Jonisch, lived near us. They used to dress Ruth like a little doll, with navy bows in her hair and gray dresses made from thick, rich wool with wide black buttons down the back. Uncle Sam and his family had a successful leather tannery business that ensured Ruth would never want for bows or big-buttoned dresses. The Jonisch family wasn't rich before the war, but life was pretty comfortable.

On September 2, 1939, when Ruth was only four weeks

old, my aunt Cecia took her to a neighbor's house for a Sabbath gathering. Husbands were seated in the living room, where they talked about politics and fears of an impending war. They huddled around a radio listening to news of Germany's warning of war. Hitler announced that in response to Polish "incursions" on German territory, German soldiers would begin marching into Poland. It was frightening news, but the family assumed the Polish military would hold off any advance. Poland was ready.

After the meal was cleared, the men hurried to the synagogue across the street for prayers. The wives stayed behind, talking and catching up over black coffee and cookies in the dining room.

Aunt Cecia held the sleeping newborn baby Ruth against her body as the women talked, when suddenly an explosion tore through the home with a deafening slam. Every glass on the table broke, windows shattered, and the women were tossed to the floor as the entire house shook to its very foundation.

The house had taken a direct hit from one of the thousands of bombs dropped by German aircraft. The bomb destroyed their empty living room—but spared the dining room full of women and the newborn baby just steps away.

So Ruth's start in life was about as rocky as mine. When

we were taken outside as infants, we both must have thought it normal to see homes in partial collapse or to see angry groups of men carrying rifles and shouting orders. Our early childhood years were defined by ghetto life and while we were far too young to understand what was going on around us, we could feel the grip of our mothers' arms tighten around us every time a soldier was near.

But here's the difference between my parents and Ruth's mother and father: in 1942, when the ghetto's secret news-papers began forecasting deportations and "resettlement to the east," my uncle Sam and aunt Cecia felt certain they needed to go into hiding.

In the nearby village of Bobolice they found a farmer named Jozef Kolacz who was willing to take them in, along with several of their relatives. Jozef's farmhouse had an attic where they could sleep and set up quarters. The farm also had a secret underground bunker in case the Germans came searching and they needed another hiding place. The Jonisches and their cousins would pay Jozef monthly for the hideout. In all, ten relatives would ultimately be packed into the small attic space.

Despite the generosity, bravery, and selflessness of Jozef and his wife, Apolonia, who were willing to take the risk of hiding Jews, there was one problem. The couple insisted that Ruth could not stay. It was just too dangerous, they said, to have such a young child in the house. What if the Germans searched the home and Ruth made a noise or cried? She was a good little girl, but she was barely three years old. Even Uncle Sam and Aunt Cecia had to admit that Jozef was right to worry. German guards immediately killed all Jews they discovered in hiding. Jozef and his family could be executed, too.

So Sam and Cecia reached out to a Polish housekeeper, a maid who had worked in their home for many years. They had been good to her, paying her well and treating her kindly for a long time. She had been a trusted member of their household.

"Please," they said, "take Ruth and keep her safe for us until the war is over."

They offered the woman a very handsome sum of money, and she promised she would care for Ruth. A date was set when Uncle Sam and his teenage nephew Eli would bring Ruth from the farmhouse into town to be handed off.

Aunt Cecia knew she could not join them. She certainly couldn't stand in the center of town and coolly hand over her precious daughter to another woman, perhaps forever. She was sure she could not contain her sadness or her tears. A difficult public goodbye would have roused attention, so instead, when the day of Ruth's departure arrived, Cecia was forced to kiss her daughter farewell an hour earlier in the seclusion of the farmhouse attic.

Every relative who was present on that late fall morning would tell you that to their dying day they would be haunted by the piercing cries of Ruth as she was torn from Cecia's arms.

"Mamishu! I want to stay with you!" she begged. "Mamishu!"

As hard as Ruth cried, Aunt Cecia cried even harder—because she knew what this goodbye truly meant.

Finally, mother and distraught baby girl were separated. My uncle Sam and Eli carried Ruth all the way into town. Cecia had dressed her warmly in a navy wool overcoat, boots, and a hat for the long walk on a crisp afternoon. Shallow snowbanks lined the road, left behind from an unseasonably early storm. Uncle Sam and Eli were outside the ghetto now and had to be quick and discreet. If Germans found them here, all three would be sentenced to death.

Uncle Sam spotted his former maid as they approached the Żarki marketplace and waved her over. He handed her a large, heavy satchel of money. He kissed his only daughter one last time on the cheek before saying goodbye. Ruth's face was tear-stained but she was in shock, with no energy left to cry or to struggle.

The maid assured Uncle Sam she would take good care of Ruth. She needed only to find her brother in the crowd, as he would be coming with a wagon so that they could take the little girl to the maid's modest house on the outskirts of town.

I don't know what it was—a hunch, maybe, a gut feeling. But as the maid and Ruth walked away, Ruth's cousin Eli suddenly felt certain that something was amiss. He convinced his uncle to follow the woman. It wasn't safe to stay in town much longer, but Eli was insistent.

Keeping their distance, they watched as the young woman ducked in and out of the crowd, pulling Ruth along by the hand. The maid didn't appear to be looking for anyone. Instead, it seemed as though she was trying to disappear from view. Finally, when she thought she was safely out of sight, the woman pulled Ruth to the side of the road, plunked her down in a small bank of soft white snow, and walked away.

In disbelief, Uncle Sam wove his way through townspeople and hurried to his daughter, who was again in tears. He lifted her up and hugged her to his chest as snow slid off her wet boots onto his clothing.

Meantime, Eli chased down the maid, who was already

dodging through the crowd. When he finally caught up to her, he demanded the money be returned. After much debate she did indeed hand over the satchel—and the two men returned to the farmhouse hours later, with little Ruth asleep in her daddy's arms.

You can imagine the reunion.

Aunt Cecia hugged and kissed her daughter's face and hands, and for many nights to come Ruth would sleep against her mother's body in the farmhouse attic. Relatives lying just feet away in that hideout would remember hearing Ruth mutter in her sleep at night, "Mami, I won't leave you. I won't ever leave you."

But of course, Ruth had to leave. The situation remained the same. It was too risky to hide a small child in the farmhouse.

Ruth's family was acquainted with a Catholic shoemaker in town named Boyanek who had five boys. When Ruth was born, Boyanek often joked with Uncle Sam, "What my wife wouldn't give for just one little girl like that!"

It was a long shot, but the Jonisches and their relatives decided to contact Boyanek. They were stunned when he and his wife instantly said yes—they would take Ruth in and raise her as their own.

Uncle Sam was wholeheartedly relieved, but both he and Aunt Cecia knew this meant another painful goodbye.

Cecia simply could not bear another parting like the last one. She knew that Ruth would scream and cry, dig her tiny fingers into her mother's forearm, and beg to stay.

So Aunt Cecia arranged to obtain a bottle of sleeping pills. She broke one pill in half, dissolved it into Ruth's thin soup at dinnertime, and with bittersweet relief stroked her daughter's back until my little cousin closed her eyes.

Uncle Sam and Eli waited until they felt certain Ruth was fast asleep. And then carefully, quietly they lifted the little girl off Aunt Cecia's chest. Before they could carry her down the ladder that led from the attic, however, Ruth awoke screaming and begged to stay with her mother. It was as though she knew she would be taken away again; clearly, no sleeping pill in the world was as powerful as Ruth's longing to be with her mother. My cousin was far too young to understand what her parents knew all too well—that being taken away from her family might be her only chance for survival.

Finally, Eli and Uncle Sam were able to pull Ruth downstairs, where Boyanek was waiting to bring home his "new little girl." She was still crying hysterically, but there was no energy left in her body to kick and fight.

The first few days of the transition were hard on everyone. Ruth cried herself to sleep alone in her new twin bed.

Boyanek's wife fretted over whether this child could ever love her new mother. Incredibly, however, Ruth managed to assimilate into her new home fairly quickly. She began calling Boyanek "Grandpa" (as he was older), and she called his wife "Auntie."

Within a few weeks, Ruth came to adore them both. She was very bright and she soon learned to speak perfect Polish. Until then, she had mostly used the colloquial Jewish language of Yiddish. The family began calling their new little girl "Kristina"—a more suitable name for a Catholic child.

One Monday evening after the sun had set, there was an unexpected knock at the Boyaneks' door. Ruth's smile instantly disappeared and her face paled. She had been warned to run and hide immediately if there was ever an unplanned visitor at the house. Ruth scrambled like a jackrabbit under Auntie's bed, closing her eyes and covering her ears.

After a few moments came the faint rumble of several men talking in the hallway.

"It's all right," Boyanek called. "You can come out, my little sweetheart."

But Ruth did not come out. She stayed still as stone for what seemed like a very long time as the men searched from room to room.

Ruth had been told that whenever she hid herself she was not to come out, even if she was being asked to do so, until the unexpected visitors left. The Germans kept a careful accounting of who lived in each household, and if a little girl suddenly appeared amid the band of five Boyanek brothers, the ruse would be over. Soldiers were notorious for leaving no stone unturned in their home searches and often spoke in soft sweet voices, coaxing Jewish children to come out of their hiding places. "It's safe," they would say in broken Yiddish. "Come out, little one."

Finally, Ruth uncovered her ears enough to hear something familiar in these men's voices. She let out a giggle from under the bed. Two large heads soon appeared in view, and she stuck her tongue out at them. It was her favorite big cousin, Eli, and her beloved uncle Mullek (another of my mother's brothers). They had snuck out of the farmhouse attic to check on Ruth, and to deliver hugs from her parents and a payment to Boyanek.

After that, Ruth's cousin Eli visited regularly to see how she was faring and to drop off money for Boyanek. It was relatively easy for him to sneak through town unnoticed because he did not look like a typical Jew, with his blue eyes and blond curls. To further conceal his identity, Eli would sometimes borrow dress aprons and scarves from the farmer's wife and disguise himself as a poor farm maiden as he strolled into the square.

Aunt Cecia always waited eagerly back at the attic hide-out for updates on her daughter. Was she eating? Was she growing? Did she look happy? Cecia clung to every word of these regular updates.

The arrangement seemed to be working seamlessly until one day when some terrible news spread across town. A Catholic family not far from the Boyaneks' home had been hiding a family of Jews. Once the Nazis learned of this, the occupants in the home—the Jews and the Catholic family members alike—were all lined up against a wall and shot execution-style.

The news chilled Boyanek's wife to her bones. She tried to shake her fear, as she did care very much for Ruth, but she couldn't stop thinking about what happened to her Catholic neighbors.

The next time Uncle Mullek and Eli went to check on little Ruth, she was gone. Boyanek hung his head low as he stood in the doorway of his home and explained that his wife had become too afraid to keep Ruth any longer. Although they had tried to find her another home, they ultimately had failed.

Boyanek said he had taken Ruth a few days earlier to the much larger town of Częstochowa, to the north of Żarki, and left her on a bench in front of an orphanage associated with the famed Jasna Góra Monastery. He said he told Ruth that she had to stay right there, that "Grandpa" would be back and would bring candy for her. He knew that Ruth was such a good listener she would obey. He felt certain she had remained there long enough for a nun from the orphanage to come and find this lovely child, freshly bathed and dressed in her pretty white dress with pink and green flowers. It was a dress Cecia had sewn for Ruth by hand before they said their awful goodbyes, and it was Ruth's absolute favorite.

That's the news Uncle Mullek and Eli had to report when they snuck back to the farmhouse on leaden feet that night. Cecia said nothing as she listened. She had no words. She simply sat and ran her fingers over a piece of the floral fabric she had used to make that special dress for Ruth. She rubbed the soft cotton scrap between her thumb and her index finger, and cried.

Uncle Sam's heart was filled with anger. He could not fathom someone leaving his beloved girl on a bench in a foreign town outside a church orphanage, and he imagined every kind of terrifying outcome.

In Częstochowa, Ruth did sit and wait. After a long while, a cleaning woman outside the chapel noticed her there. Ruth had been so tired she had curled up on the bench, rested her head on her hands, and closed her sad brown eyes. That's how the cleaning woman found her, half-asleep, alone on a bench.

The Mother Superior was quickly alerted, and the two scooped Ruth right up off that bench and took her into their care. The nuns guessed that Ruth was Jewish—probably orphaned when her parents were shot by German soldiers or marched off to camps. The Mother Superior brought her inside, and Ruth soon called the orphanage home. She told them her name was Kristina, and she grew to love her peers and her caretakers.

My cousin looked different from many of the other children there, though. Like many Jews, she had big brown eyes, hair as black as night, and a darker complexion than the average Polish gentile.

Ruth's dark skin worried the nuns. German soldiers had taken over the orphanage's main building to use as a base, so soldiers were everywhere. The nuns feared that Ruth's olive skin and dark hair would give away her secret, so they kept a scarf over her head at all times.

Soon Ruth forgot all about her parents. The nuns and the children at the orphanage became her family, and she was learning to be a good Catholic child. Over time, she was even taught by the nuns to speak badly of Jews. They did this to protect her, so she would fit in and not be discovered as Jewish herself.

It was, perhaps, just easier for Ruth to believe that she belonged to the nuns and that no mother or father would ever knock on the big, wooden door to the orphanage asking if a little girl with black hair and dark-as-night eyes had been left outside the church's walls.

10

LAST-CHANCE DECISIONS

The bitter morning in October 1942 when he was greeted on the street by Officer Schmitt marked a day my father would never forget.

Schmitt had appeared without warning, his thick-gloved fingers digging firmly into Papa's forearm. As my father later told Mamishu, the smell of stale cigarettes and vodka on the officer's breath was as vile as the words he spoke. Usually, these two men could negotiate rationally and spoke to each other as though they were almost on equal footing. Papa's access to Judenrat funds had made it so. This meeting was clearly different.

Schmitt explained that he had orders to make Żarki *Judenrein* (clean of Jews). The remaining members of the Jewish community would be resettled "somewhere safe," he assured Papa. The Judenrat could choose thirty men to stay behind to clean up and to work odd jobs. The rest would be transported by sundown that same day on trains headed east.

As council president, Papa never allowed himself to cry or break down, even on the darkest days in the ghetto. And yet on this day, it was like a dam had given way and he was powerless to stop the rush of anguish. The tears seemed to clear his focus and my father suddenly saw Żarki in a way he had not seen it just one day earlier.

Hurrying along a cobblestoned street, still headed to the library for a meeting with the council, he passed the Brachmans' house. He noticed for the first time a spot in the roadway where the stones were stained dark red with blood. It was undoubtedly the blood of an innocent Jew, beaten at the hands of a Nazi. Perhaps a Jewish man had tripped while carrying a backbreaking load, or a mother had been holding a child whose crying annoyed a German guard. Either way, Papa had walked this street a hundred times and missed the markings of terror in this one particular spot.

As he walked on, he was again ashamed as he took note of bullet holes in the front door of the Akermans' apartment house.

His friend Benyamin waved to him along the way, and for the first time Papa noticed that Benyamin's skin had yellowed from malnutrition and that the young man, only in his twenties, now walked with a limp.

How foolish Papa felt for looking right past all the misery and blindly believing, for three straight years, that the end of the war was near. How ignorant to think America's entrance into the war would stop a powerful dictator's plans. How silly of him to imagine that he could fight the rolling tide of Hitler's evil plans with a small-scale bribery scheme and a cordial relationship with a local German officer.

In truth, that hopefulness Papa had maintained made life tolerable for himself, for Mamishu and Bobeshi, and especially for Samuel and me. But at that moment, he wished he had seen Żarki all along for what it was—a piteous ghetto full of Jews with blue stars on their sleeves and bull's-eyes on their backs.

Papa began the meeting with his council by speaking in a slow, controlled voice: "The time has come for every Jewish man and woman in Żarki to protect themselves and make their own decisions about where to turn next. The Judenrat can do no more. This town is to become *Judenrein*."

There was a collective gasp. Then silence.

Of the thirty-four hundred people who once filled

Żarki's Jewish quarter, more than two thousand had escaped or gone into hiding, with help from the Judenrat. At least six hundred had been killed, or had died from the scarcity of food and medicine. The eight hundred remaining—including my family and me—now seemed doomed.

"We still have money, we still have gold," Papa said, when he finally found his voice again at the meeting. "We saved those funds for a reason."

"Officer Schmitt? The soldiers? Where do we go? What can we even ask for? They have their orders," one councilman said.

The group was silent. Everyone knew these might be the last decisions they made.

"A larger work crew!" Papa shouted. "Schmitt said we will be allowed to keep a few men, maybe thirty, to empty homes and deliver valuables left behind to the German government. We'll tell them we need one hundred people."

Lejzer Steinem snapped, "And send seven hundred to Treblinka? Send our families to that place that smells of burning flesh?" He was shouting, too.

"What choice do we have? We can't overturn an order of the German government. No soldier or officer in town has the ranking to do such a thing. Saving everyone would be—"

BAM! BAM!

The men froze in place. The sound of gunshots, not far away, left them cold and silent.

BAM! BAM! BAM! More gunshots—the beginning of many they would hear that day.

There was chaos outside the windows as panicked neighbors ran into their homes, wondering what was happening.

I will tell you what was happening. On October 6, 1942, German soldiers lightened their load. Instead of transporting and "resettling" all eight hundred Jewish residents of Żarki, they got rid of more than a hundred people the easy way: they shot them.

Some were accused of trying to escape (and in truth, some were trying to escape). Some were killed for no reason at all. They were just marched to the Jewish cemetery, lined up, and executed.

The first sounds of gunfire outside only fueled Papa's insistence. "We cannot save everyone. But surely we can save more than the Germans would like."

With little time left to act, the council agreed. Papa would talk to Schmitt. The council would await word. First

Papa raced home to bring the news to Mamishu and my grandmother.

"Sophie, I need you to find your brothers and talk to them immediately. If they plan to go into hiding, this is their last chance." Mullek and Moniek had already chosen secure attics in town in which to hide if the Żarki ghetto was closed. David and his wife, Gutia, would be staying with Sam and Cecia in Jozef Kolacz's farmhouse attic.

Mamishu blinked away tears, finding strength for Papa. "I will speak to them now. But, Israel, what about us? The boys? Your mother?"

"Sophie, we're going to stay. I think we can stay."

"What?" Mamishu was incredulous. "I don't understand."

"I'm going to speak with Schmitt. Please, Soph, I'm asking you to put your trust in me. I don't know what is best, but I think I can persuade Schmitt to leave us here, in our home, at least for now."

"And my mother? My father? They don't have the strength to hide in an attic," she said softly.

"I'll do what I can, Sophie."

Mamishu did not argue or second-guess him. She kissed my father on the cheek and nodded toward the door. "Go, then. I'll send word to my family and wait for you here," she said.

For the second time that day, Mamishu watched her husband out the front window of their home and wondered if it would be the last time she would see him.

Papa hurried to the old bootmaker's shop, where he suspected Officer Schmitt would be finalizing plans and organizing his men to launch the formal deportation of Jews. He was right.

By now, the soldiers were acquainted with my father, so they did not raise their guns when they saw him hustling into the Gestapo base, the door slamming shut behind him.

"Officer Schmitt, I have some information to share with you," Papa said with a glance that indicated, *We should speak in private.* They stepped outside the back door of the old shop into an alleyway.

"This is an order directly from Nazi regional headquarters, Bornstein," Schmitt said before Papa even spoke. "The town *will* be made *Judenrein.*"

"Yes, I understand. That's not why I'm here." Papa looked down nervously. He had always asked questions on behalf of the community. His first question that day, however, was completely self-motivated. No request had ever meant more to him. "My family—my wife, my mother, and my two boys, Samuel and Michael—they need to stay here with me while I oversee cleanup. I have come with banknotes, of course."

Papa pulled Judenrat funds from his two pockets, and Schmitt grabbed the money with his black-gloved hands.

"I can accommodate that request," Officer Schmitt said as he folded the banknotes neatly and tucked them in the chest pocket of his uniform shirt. "They can stay back with the work crew."

My father continued nervously, "One more request, Officer Schmitt. The work crew is simply too small. You know there are many valuables to be found here in basement vaults and underground hiding places. There are also bodies to be buried and much cleanup to do."

Papa was about to ask that one hundred people be left behind. Then he thought about each of those hundred lives. Just as Lejzer Steinem had argued, each person sent away could be a life destroyed. As the words rolled off his tongue, my father increased the number.

"No fewer than one hundred fifty people could do the job. Officer Schmitt, please allow me the larger work crew I need."

Officer Schmitt threw his head back with laughter. Still smiling a wicked smile, he said, "You are a man of great earnestness. I should have guessed you'd be here begging!

You may keep one hundred twenty people, and not one more. The rest will be leaving promptly from the Złoty Potok railroad station. Make your list."

Papa thanked Officer Schmitt, but as he turned to walk down the narrow alley toward the street, the Gestapo leader grabbed my father by the arm and stopped him.

"Tell your people, they're to gather in the square by five o'clock this evening. Anyone not present will be found and killed." Schmitt leaned in close. "I promise you, Herr Bornstein, my men *will* find every last Jew. They'll enjoy bringing them to me."

Papa forced himself not to swallow or blink. "Yes, of course. I'll see to it that everyone is there."

My father raced back to the library to inform his council, who practically cheered when they heard that 120 people could stay behind in the ghetto. Within seconds, though, their expressions fell and their faces went white. The realization sank in. They would now have to choose who stayed behind. Those not chosen would be sent to the camps where chimneys puffed the foul smoke of human flesh.

They sat at the library table where they had studied the Torah and dissected great poetry in days gone by, and now scribbled names onto paper. Two lists: one list of those who would stay, and one of those who would board trains before sundown.

The list included the names of many friends in the close-knit community.

Writing down the names of Esther and Mordecai Jonisch, though, pained my father more than any other single decision. He was sending away his own in-laws, Mamishu's parents. How many nights had he sat at their dining room table celebrating the Sabbath? How gracious was Mordecai on the night Israel's parents had asked to arrange a marriage for him and Sophie? How patient and loving was Esther with her grandsons? What kind of man sends away his wife's parents?

"There's no argument to be made for keeping them here to work," his Judenrat committee members had implored him. "The Germans will send them away no matter what—they are old now. And the soldiers will punish you for trying to keep them here."

The men were right.

"And, Israel—Sophie's parents may well find safety at the camps."

There was no reasonable argument Papa could make to the contrary.

My father truly did not know what lay at the end of the tracks, but if the underground papers had their facts straight, no one who boarded those trains would return. Still, Papa was hopeful that his wife's parents and all the others who were stuffed aboard the freight cars would find some refuge at the end of the line until the war ended.

My uncles were probably already fleeing for their secret hideouts right then. But my father did add the names of many of his own friends and relatives to the list of those to keep behind for cleanup in Żarki.

After the war, I asked a survivor from town if Papa was a traitor for helping German soldiers choose their trainloads and for choosing to spare his relatives.

"If there are ten people standing next to you—five are neighbors, five are your family—and you are asked to choose half to be killed, whom do you choose?" the man asked me.

"I understand," I said. "That's not an easy decision."

The survivor snapped back at me, "Of course it's an easy decision," he said. "You choose your family first. Your father did what he had to do. He was human."

After speedy debate in a room filled with untold sadness, the list was complete. Papa and his twenty Judenrat committee members raced across the ghetto, telling those chosen to leave to be at the market square by five o'clock. Many said they wouldn't be there. They would risk an escape. Papa wished every man and woman well and warned them soldiers would be looking for them.

*   *   *

At that late afternoon hour on October 6, 1942, hundreds of Jewish men, women, and children gathered nervously in Żarki's Jewish square, one suitcase apiece in hand. They then began a long march to the Złoty Potok train station twelve kilometers away. The young and the very old boarded carriages to take them there. Those on foot were whipped with leather straps if they moved too slow or were clubbed in the back if they appeared to stray.

Finally at the train station, healthy, active young parents were separated from their children and boarded trains for work camps, where they could pack ammunition, make weapons and tools, or build roads for the German government. Young children and senior citizens were chosen for a separate train. They would go to Treblinka, the death camp.

As the selection took place, children clung to mothers' skirts, begging to stay with them. Fathers wept and gave hugs that must have carried the weight of a thousand bedtimes. They knew there might be no bedtime hugs again. Mothers kissed every corner of babies' faces—chins, temples, and cheeks—breathing in the smell of sweet, sticky skin and hoping to always remember the scent.

But it wasn't the scent these mothers would remember

most. The sound of their children screaming "Mamishu! I want Mami!" would haunt their memories instead.

My own papa would hear ghosts screaming those words, too, as he walked from house to empty house, collecting valuables. He carried a steel rod and was expected to pierce holes in the soil behind homes, looking for hidden treasures. But he never checked cellar compartments and ignored soft spots in backyards. He would just hop over those places and carry on with his work.

Papa soon learned that Grandma Esther and Grandpa Mordecai had been deported to Treblinka. They weren't young enough for heavy labor. I wonder if my grandmother wore a pretty dress for the ride, hopeful she could keep something special. She was spotted once at the camp, but then never seen again. Word got back to Żarki that my grandfather didn't even make it all the way to Treblinka. He died from suffocation on the hot, cramped cattle car with so little ventilation.

I can't pretend to know how Papa shared this news with my mother or how she reconciled the fact that he had sent them away. I know there was heartbreak. Mordecai and Esther Jonisch were models of love, faith, and family.

Mamishu and her six siblings adored their parents with their whole hearts.

And here was my mother, left behind in a ghetto that was now a virtual ghost town. Empty homes lined every street in the Jewish quarter of Żarki.

Sometimes at night, you might see the dim light of a candle in an attic where someone was risking survival. The 120-person work crew was thinned to fifty in a matter of months, as Officer Schmitt carried out new orders.

Papa pushed again for more help. Ruth's uncle Moshe Zborowski, the wealthy and generous man who had once paid for secret schooling of children in the ghetto, snuck back into town one night. He had escaped the ghetto just before it was liquidated. His own children were in hiding, but with nowhere safe to go for himself, he returned hoping to find refuge in Żarki. Papa once again compelled Officer Schmitt to increase the cleanup crew, allowing Moshe to stay.

Mamishu, Bobeshi, Samuel, and I were among only a few Jews left in town who weren't on the work detail. That year of my life, I saw few other children. We stayed inside most days, and Bobeshi cooked or tidied up while my mother schooled my brother and me and tried to give us a sense of routine and normalcy. It wasn't so bad, I guess—except things were about to change again.

11

TRAPPED

The men dragged out the work for many months. Every morning, they formed a straight line outside the main synagogue, where soldiers checked a list and accounted for every person. Some were assigned to work in Jewish businesses that had been taken away from their owners. The men were also given orders to build a large stable for horses, and that work delayed them even longer.

Spring came, then summer. On August 5, 1943, the work crew in Żarki had just finished building the stable and was hoping to get a new project soon.

"I'll have some fresh cabbage soup ready for you when you get home tonight," Mamishu told Papa as we all walked to the synagogue for the morning head count. The street was quiet, as it always was—only a few men from the work detail were ahead of us.

Mamishu squeezed my hand tightly when we approached.

It was strange to see five Gestapo officers outside and even more strange that they were shuffling everyone inside the building. It was a beautiful summer morning. There would be no reason to move us indoors for the count.

Officer Schmitt appeared just as we approached. Papa started to ask him something, but the officer just held up his hand, warning my father to stop.

Papa knew when to hold his tongue. We walked into the synagogue, passing a stone in front of the doorway that used to carry an engraved inscription with words from the Torah. Vandals had chiseled out the Hebrew message long ago.

"Ton mir bakumen tsu helfn haynt?" I asked Mamishu excitedly. Do we get to help today? With no other children in Żarki anymore, days were long and Samuel and I were often bored.

"Sha, sha!" my mother said, putting her finger to her lips and warning me to stay quiet.

After what felt like a very long wait, Officer Schmitt finally entered the synagogue.

"New orders for you today," he barked in German. "You won't be needed here any longer."

Everyone in the room exchanged terrified stares.

"You'll be heading to the ghetto at Radomsko. Do not worry, gentlemen. They will take good care of you there."

No one felt comforted. Several refugees from Radomsko, a town north of Częstochowa, had snuck into Żarki to hide in attics over the last twelve months. They brought horrifying news. Trains came almost weekly to Radomsko to carry Jewish prisoners to Treblinka. There, they were being killed in gas chambers on arrival.

Schmitt continued, "So you will wait here until we have enough vehicles ready to carry you all to Radomsko."

With that, the Gestapo members we had seen outside carried in pails of water and a few loaves of bread and then they boarded up the doors of the synagogue, trapping us all inside.

Mamishu cried, "We should have left, Israel! Why didn't we sneak away? Why didn't we hide like my brothers? My sisters are gone! My parents are gone! And now we wait here for our own death?"

She was sobbing, and Samuel and I were no doubt very scared at seeing everyone in such a panic. Papa tried to calm her down, stroking her soft, wavy blond hair and promising her we would find our way, but Mamishu was inconsolable.

One night went by and no one returned for us. Papa was wise enough to know the bread and water might need to last, so he parceled it out in very small rations. I begged for more in the morning, but Papa wouldn't relent.

Some people tried to escape. Moshe Zborowski climbed the stairs to the second floor of the synagogue, opened a window, and jumped into the Nysa Łużycka River just below. Two men in the work detail followed him right out the window.

Jumping into the river was an impossible option for my family. Papa was the only one among us who even knew how to swim. We later learned the plan failed for Moshe Zborowski. He was believed to have been spotted by a Polish informer as he floated downriver, then was shot and killed.

After three days of sleeping on the floor of the hot synagogue, we heard people pulling the boards off the front door. Fresh air blew in as the doors opened and a line of Gestapo officers entered, guns drawn.

Then came Officer Schmitt. "Trucks are on their way to collect you. You have thirty minutes to go home, fill a bag with your belongings, and return here. Do not think of running. As you know, we will find you," he said, as though this were a game.

Mamishu, worn and tired, picked me up so we could rush faster. The five of us—including my mother, father, brother, and grandmother—hurried to the house to collect our things. My parents and grandmother started in my parents' bedroom, and Samuel and I stayed close.

"Sophie, the money and jewels in the backyard!" Papa said suddenly. "We may need them for barter."

"Israel, you know the war will be ending soon, and then what? We need to leave something here. Something for the future."

"The future?" My father was confused. "We need to live past today first, Soph! Do you not understand? They're turning people into *soap* in the camps. The rumors say they're burning bodies, melting down human fat, and turning Jews into bars of wax and soap!"

"Oh, I'd be a lovely bar of soap, don't you think, Israel? Lavender, for sure! Or maybe lilac and rosehips?" Mamishu said with an anxious smile. "My perfumed skin would make for the perfect ingredient." She was trying to calm my father with humor, however awkward the attempt.

When my mother was panicked, my father always stayed calm. In this case, the reverse was true.

"Israel, we *do* have money with us already," she reminded him.

Papa had some gold stashed in the hollow heels of his shoes and more banknotes in his shoulder pads. Mamishu had sewn a special lining in her skirt and stashed money in it, and Bobeshi, too, had a similar insurance policy sewn into her clothing.

Papa relaxed just a little bit. He even smiled when he looked down at Mamishu's bulging gray suitcase on the floor. It was so full it didn't quite zip closed, and a piece of bright yellow floral fabric stuck out at the corner. Papa's beloved Sophie couldn't even make a high-stakes wartime journey without a cheery dress in her bag. He guessed there was some rouge buried in the suitcase, too, and he kissed Mamishu on her pink cheek as they continued to discuss their plans.

"*Sha!*" they heard Bobeshi shout from the second bedroom. "I hear something, Israel!"

There was a noise. Everyone stopped and strained their ears.

Creak. There was definitely a noise. Footsteps! Someone was in the house.

12

THE PARTING GIFT

There was nowhere to hide. Papa knew it was too late to run. Someone was in the house, and it was likely an armed Gestapo member coming to drag us to the cemetery. Maybe he wouldn't even bother with that. Maybe he would execute us right there in our bedrooms.

Mamishu slipped her diamond wedding ring under her tongue. I'd often seen her do so when soldiers and officers were near.

Suddenly, Officer Schmitt's large, dark figure appeared in my parents' bedroom doorway. He was such a tall man that his spiked hair nearly touched the molding at the top of the entrance.

Papa relaxed just a little. "Officer Schmitt, you said we have thirty minutes. I have no watch anymore, but it couldn't have been more than ten?"

"Why so defensive?" Schmitt asked. "I've come to help you."

My father was silent. He no doubt considered pulling some gold coins from his shoe, but then he knew Schmitt would take it all. He would find the banknotes in his suit's shoulder pads. There would be nothing left for the next portion of the journey. So my father just listened.

"Bornstein, you and your family will not be joining your comrades in Radomsko."

My parents exchanged a look of confusion.

"Your family will be leaving in your own truck. You are going two hundred kilometers northeast to work at the ammunitions factory in Pionki. I requested that they put you and your wife to work there indefinitely. Your mother and your sons will accompany you."

Officer Schmitt gave my mother a proud nod as if to say, *I know. I'm a good man. I'm a good man.*

It was a parting gift from the German guard who carried just a little bit of guilt at exterminating thousands from this town. Inside the crisply ironed uniform shirts of the men who marched like robots, I suppose there were still beating hearts.

We didn't know how big a gift this was until we arrived at Pionki. In comparison to ghetto life in Żarki, Pionki was a virtual heaven. The biggest improvement by far was the food. In the ghetto we were practically starving. Prisoners at Pionki probably had fuller bellies than any other Jews in Poland.

Papa and Mamishu worked alongside Christian Poles who came to the gunpowder manufacturing facility for paid work. The factory was the largest of its kind in all of Poland.

"Can you get me three pounds of beef brisket in exchange for this link of gold?" Papa whispered one morning to the Polish man who worked alongside him at the factory. The man had smiled at my father many times and made it clear that he did not mind working with a Jew.

"Of course, my friend. You look hungry. I'll make it four pounds."

The two needn't have whispered. These kinds of deals were made all day long at Pionki.

The head of the factory was Hauptmann Brendt, a German civilian engineer. (In German, *Hauptmann* is a term of respect ascribed to leaders.) He imposed a heavy workload— twelve hours on your feet with only one significant break for lunch. But Hauptmann Brendt never treated prisoners cruelly. In fact, he was credited with saving prisoners' lives on more than one occasion. The guards who monitored the factory followed his lead.

And the Christians who worked in the factory either were affected by Hauptmann Brendt's kindness or were softhearted, too. They often brought food to share with prisoners during workshifts.

"Israel, the son I love so dear, you spoil us!" Bobeshi cried when Papa entered our room the next night, holding up the largest piece of meat anyone had seen in years. I had never tasted such a delicacy—at least I couldn't remember such a burst of flavors and juices like that. Bread and potatoes tasted flat and dry by comparison.

"How did we get so fortunate?" Mamishu smiled, looking out the window. Oh yes! There were windows in most rooms at Pionki. We had our own twelve-by-twelve living space, which fit two bunk beds. And the window overlooked majestic scenery. If you think the factory town of Pionki was cold and sparse—oh no, it was actually buried in a forest of lush green leaves that were fast becoming red-orange.

The Jewish encampment was surrounded by barbed-wire fencing, but that was easy to overlook. No soldiers patrolled the barracks. There were seldom inspections at all. If there had been, Samuel and I might have been sent away. Young children were only unofficially allowed at Pionki. If no one spoke up, no one got sent away. By and large, the thousand or so Jews at the camp were incredibly supportive of one another.

We ate our dinner of meat and nutrient-rich sweet potatoes sitting in a circle on the floor of our room. Papa knocked on doors in the hall to share some of the abundance. We had made friends quickly on the third floor of the barracks.

Bobeshi, her joints too stiff to allow her to sit cross-legged on the floor with the rest of us, ate her meal sitting on the straw-filled mattress on the lower bunk bed. She licked her fingers clean when she was done—something I had never seen my meticulous grandmother do before.

Then Mamishu and Papa set to work on their second-shift job: the education of my brother and me.

My father had collected rocks, sticks, leaves, and chestnuts on his walk home to the barracks that evening, so he was prepared. He laid eight small chestnuts on the floor in a loose pile.

"Samuel," he said, "if there are three squirrels coming over for dinner, and each one will need two chestnuts to nibble—how many of these chestnuts should we set out, and how many will be left over?"

Samuel looked confused.

"Multiplication," Papa reminded him gently.

Carefully my father moved the chestnuts into three

equal piles, with two pieces still left in the middle of the floor.

Samuel eventually got it.

Papa pulled six rocks from his pocket and set them on the floor. Before he could begin assigning a problem, Samuel pulled two rocks from the pile and held them up to the light at the window. Then he stuffed them in his pocket.

"How about we do the next one with sticks instead?" Papa asked.

While my father and big brother practiced arithmetic, Mamishu was snuggled next to me in the bed I shared at night with Samuel, practicing my Hebrew alphabet. She exaggerated every letter sound as we walked through the ancient symbols like we did together every evening. I was getting good at sounding out words already. During the day, to keep occupied, Samuel would read to me until he was hoarse. Mamishu was proud of us. She didn't have much of a formal education herself, but she did value learning almost as much as she valued our faith.

Friday nights in the camp, my parents and grandmother would teach me new prayers and Jewish songs. Papa would raise his hand high in the air, grasping the stem of an imaginary kiddush cup.

"*Baruch atah Adonai, Eloheinu melech haolam, borei p'ri*

hagafen." We praise you, Eternal God, sovereign of the universe, who creates the fruit of the vine.

After we recited the blessing over the fake wine, we passed the fake cup among us, pretending to take sips. I thought that was very funny.

Mamishu still dreamed of a day when we would celebrate the Sabbath together back in our own home in Żarki, the five of us singing and enjoying challah and roasted chicken and raising the silver kiddush cup that now lay underground, tucked away in our old backyard.

For now, the routine of work and life at Pionki was the family's new normal existence. Mamishu and Papa went to work seven days a week, helping to create the very bullets that would kill our own people.

It's a shame we hadn't arrived at Pionki sooner. Those who arrived earlier in the war were given jobs in camp administration. Camp administrators had shorter shifts working in an office and handling paperwork for the camp. They saw to it that factory jobs were all filled with qualified laborers. They made sure toiletries, food, and water were brought into camp regularly. They sat at desks.

Papa and Mamishu were on their feet all day, but they never complained. That is, until about six months after their arrival, when a new *Werkschutzleiter* (factory manager), Herr Widner, was assigned to Pionki. Although he didn't take the place of Hauptmann Brendt, Herr Widner now managed the workers. The week he arrived, my parents showed their first signs of panic. They weren't alone.

At first, rules just became stricter. No one left a work shift ten minutes early without being flogged with a whip. There were no excuses for being late and no special permission to stay back if you were sick.

"What in heaven's name is that?" Mamishu stopped to stare at something just outside the barracks one morning in early summer of 1944.

Their shift was starting soon, and Papa tried to lead her by the hand.

Then he saw what she saw.

In the courtyard of our living quarters, where families gathered to relax and talk at night, stood a strange contraption: two wooden posts in the ground about ten feet apart, with a wooden beam connecting them at the top. There were two ropes hanging from the beam with large loops at the end of each. A gallows! Someone might as well have been sitting there with a gun pointed at my parents' heads.

The message was the same: *If you make a mistake, you will hang!*

Herr Widner had arranged to have the gallows set up there. Overnight, announcements were posted around the camp. They warned that any Jew who tried to desert, or leave camp without permission, would be caught and hanged. If a person successfully got away, another innocent person would hang in his or her place.

It did not take long before the new rule was put to the test.

A man desperate to reach his family at another camp snuck out of the barracks late one night. A search party looked for him, but he was not found. Instead, Herr Widner ordered that a floormate be hanged. The new manager was eager to show he meant business. Terror went through the camp.

But here is how I know that one man or woman alone can make a difference. Hauptmann Brendt intervened. With nothing to gain from it, he stepped in and told Herr Widner he would not allow his worker to be executed for committing no crime. The hanging was canceled.

Sadly, on another occasion, five deserters were caught. This time, Hauptmann Brendt had no argument to make. These men were guilty. The entire camp was forced to watch as those five people were hanged by their necks in the courtyard. Guards warned that if any prisoners looked away, even turned their eyes downward during the execution, they would be whipped. As an "unofficial guest" in the Pionki barracks, I managed to stay back during that event.

It was a scary time in Pionki. But no time was scarier than the July afternoon when Hauptmann Brendt brought his radio onto the floor of the factory. The reports were in German, but the factory leader repeated what was being said slowly so that everyone could understand. In a sorrowful and apologetic voice, he shared the news. The Pionki labor camp was being shut down. Jews would be "resettled" to Auschwitz. When Papa returned to our room that night, he told Bobeshi. He didn't even have enough faith or courage left to say what he always tried to believe: *Gam ze ya'avor.*

13

B-1148

"I can't swallow, Papa. Are we almost there?"

I was desperately thirsty on the train ride to Auschwitz. The journey was something like three hundred kilometers from Pionki. We had been traveling for at least a day. There weren't windows in the train car, but there was enough of a crack between the sliding wooden doors to see a sliver of light. Night had come and gone at least once—maybe twice. I couldn't wait for the train to finally stop. The container of water Papa had snuck on board had long since been drained. He probably regretted sharing it with others.

"I don't think it will be much longer. I'm sure there will be water and food waiting for us, *zeisele*," Papa said.

"Oh, yes! There will be noodle kugel and potato pancakes stacked to the ceiling," said the man behind us. "Just don't forget to wipe your mouth with a napkin before they make you disappear forever."

"Disappear?" Samuel asked.

"Don't listen to crazy people," Mamishu muttered. "He's just blathering about nonsense."

We couldn't miss the way she glowered at the man, who was jammed up against Papa's back because of the lack of space.

I really didn't give the older passenger's comment much thought once my parents dismissed it. I was too thirsty to think about anything other than what it would feel like to have just one droplet of water spill down my throat, so that I could properly swallow. My tongue nearly stuck to my teeth.

It was a hot July in Poland. On board the train, everyone's body was touching somebody else's, we were so close together. I was soaked with sweat and urine. There was no bathroom on board, so there was no other way. The smells were simply grotesque.

"It's all right," Bobeshi had comforted me when I first realized my pants were soaked. Her hair, wet with perspiration, was matted down and stuck to the sides of her face. I had never seen her look so disheveled.

The train moved so slowly on its tracks, it was hard to

believe we would get anywhere. Samuel was queasy from the train's constant rocking rhythm, the smells, and the awkward position he was forced into on the overstuffed freight car—and he finally gave in to tears.

To comfort him, Mamishu softly sang, *"Zog nit keinmal als du gehnest dem letzen veg..."* Don't say this is your last journey. This is not your last path . . .

This was the first verse of what had become known as "The Ghetto Song." She pulled the bangs from Samuel's eyes. His hair had grown long at Pionki, where we had no scissors. Layers of brown hair always seemed to cover his face. Mamishu wanted to see those eyes right now, though. As she wiped his tears she kept on singing, though she slurred the words. "Don't thay this is your lath journey. Thisth isth not your lasth path . . ." It's hard to have good diction with a diamond ring hidden under your tongue.

My grandmother, who rarely sang, started humming, too. Then Papa and others joined in prayerful song. Most of the journey, though, was marked by just the sounds of coughing, moaning, and very heavy breathing.

Finally—maybe two days after the journey began—the wheels slowed and the train jerked to a stop.

Mamishu squeezed my hand as the door rattled open. Instantly we heard men barking commands in German.

"Alle raus!" they shouted. Everybody out!

The glaring sun hurt our eyes and a terrible smell attacked our noses. Just seconds before, we had been squarely focused on getting some fresh air for Samuel and some cool water for me. Suddenly, we could only think of that wretched smell, far more offensive than anything we'd endured on board the train. I don't know how to describe it. Harsh and revolting—it was the smell of burning flesh.

Even before we climbed down from the wooden boxcar, we could see a scene like nothing any of us had witnessed in the past. Hundreds of grotesquely skinny humans, with barely enough flesh to cover their bones, were lined up for what appeared to be a head count just beyond the fence. They looked straight ahead as if programmed not to move—or maybe they didn't have the energy.

Far in the distance, there was a wide chimney in the skyline that poured thick, rancid smoke into the air. Even farther away, smoke seemed to billow from other places—from more ovens to cremate the bodies of murdered prisoners, we would later learn.

In front of us, skeleton-like people swept ashes off the ground. Ashes and soot often fell over the camp like gray snow. The prisoners wore striped uniforms that hung off them like skin hangs from raw chicken. No clothes could be narrow enough to properly fit these people whose bodies were decaying, even while their hearts were still beating.

Papa slid his thin frame through the tightly packed mass of bodies disembarking from the train car and cleared a path for us. "Let's all hold hands," he said. "The guards will see we belong together and, let's hope, will bunk us as a family."

The guards were all carrying either leather whips or wooden clubs. Some had attack dogs by their side.

An older man who had made gurgling noises on the ride was now slumped in an awkward pile at the edge of the boxcar. Bobeshi rarely carried me anymore, but she snatched me up off my feet and pressed my face into her shoulder, trying to shield me from seeing what I later realized was a dead body. That man was not the only passenger who had died on the long trip. The heat, hunger, and shortage of air had claimed several lives.

Auschwitz was a monstrous complex of camps and sub-camps and it's likely we were delivered to a section called Birkenau. That means we missed seeing the infamous sign at the main gate that read ARBEIT MACHT FREI (Work makes you free). The SS guards—the elite group of German soldiers who controlled Auschwitz—wanted us to believe that if we worked hard and followed the rules, everyone would be all right.

My parents, ever optimistic, were not afraid of hard work as long as we were all together and safe.

Samuel let go of my hand for a moment and bent down to pick up a gray rock from the ground beside the train. Then he tucked it into the pocket of Mamishu's skirt as a gift.

Mamishu leaned down and kissed the top of Samuel's head. He was getting so big, and she was so short, that she barely had to bend to place a kiss on his head anymore. Then she nodded toward me to remind him to grasp my hand again. All she wanted right now was for us to stay united.

Staying together was not an option for families at Auschwitz-Birkenau, though. Speaking in the thick German tongue we had come to hate since the invasion, the guards who carried the imposing leather whips began forcing us into separate lines. Papa held up our entwined hands to show, *See! We are together. We are a family!* Mamishu and Bobeshi, too, raised their hands, clutching Samuel and me. The guards pretended they didn't even notice. They just ripped us apart and directed us to different lines.

You know that horrible feeling you get when you go somewhere and realize you have left something important behind? That's one of the feelings you got in the first sixty minutes at Auschwitz. Men reached for suitcases that weren't there. Women reached for children who had been pulled from their grip. People squinted to see and wished their eyeglasses hadn't just been taken and tossed in a pile like trash. It takes about sixty minutes to adjust and to accept that everything has just been stolen from you, even your name.

Papa and Samuel were told to stand in the men's line to get their uniforms. I was to stay with Mamishu and Bobeshi because I was so small. Young children went to the women's side of Auschwitz.

To tell the truth, young children and older prisoners often didn't stand in line for uniforms at all. They were marched straight to their death. I can't say for sure why that didn't happen to us. We were later told it was proof of miracles.

But I also wonder: Did Hauptmann Brendt—the good-hearted manager who ran the factory at Pionki—have something to do with my survival? After the war, I learned that he sent word to Auschwitz before trainloads of his workers arrived, saying that they were the best laborers in the world and that they should be kept alive and put to work.

I, of course, was far too young to be of any use. But maybe prisoners from Pionki earned some kind of special grace. Unlike those who came from other labor camps in Poland, Bobeshi wasn't frail when she arrived at the gates. At Pionki, we ate and we slept. Her health may have kept her alive.

Maybe it was part miracle and part intervention. I'll probably never know.

I do know, however, that when my mother, grandmother, and I said goodbye to Papa and Samuel at the entrance to Auschwitz, the parting was so terribly quick.

"I'll look for you later," Papa mouthed to my mother and Bobeshi.

Had we known how permanent this goodbye would be, the kiss Papa blew to Mamishu would have felt horribly insufficient. The fake nod of reassurance Mamishu gave Samuel would never have been enough.

At the front of our line a guard shuttled us into a large white room with showerheads in a long row down either side. We were told that when the doors closed, we were to clean ourselves properly and prepare to dress in uniforms.

I was the only child in sight in a room filled with undressed women, waiting for water to be turned on. I didn't understand why there was so much panic until much later.

I didn't know that many of the shower rooms at Auschwitz poured not water but, rather, deadly gas from their spouts.

There was no laughter, but there were audible sighs of relief when what came out of the showerheads was indeed water. The SS wanted this shipment of women clean and ready to work. I let the warm stream run down my body, cleaning off days of soil. I opened my mouth and let droplets pour in to wet my dry throat. Bobeshi helped me rinse my hair while Mamishu rinsed her own.

Suddenly, the water got very hot and we all scurried out from under the showerheads toward the center of the room, where SS guards and *kapos* (here meaning Jewish prisoners who had been assigned guard duty) used clubs to shove us back under the scalding water. Then the water turned icy and Mamishu grabbed me by the shoulder so that I wouldn't make the mistake of running again.

"Alle raus!" the guards shouted. The water stopped, and the guards herded everyone into another large room, where prison uniforms were handed out.

Mine was so oversized that my fingers were lost in the sleeves and the pant legs dragged along the dirty ground when I tried taking a few steps. Mamishu knelt down and rolled them at the bottom for me and then folded them once more around the waistband.

I was given wooden shoes that were about two sizes too big.

Mamishu had tossed her navy-checked skirt and carnation-yellow blouse into the pile of personal clothing, as she was instructed. It would be burned like everything else in the heap—unless a soldier rescued it to give as a gift to his wife or girlfriend.

Then we were directed to a second line, everyone still moving silently. I was hoping it was the line for cold drinking water, but I was far too small to see over the women in front of us. Mamishu was also too short to see ahead, but from the sounds of women wincing and crying we both understood this was not a line for a water well.

Tired of standing, I shifted from foot to foot, and then it was finally our turn.

"Komm her!" shouted an officer. Come here! He was pointing at me. *"Komm her!"* he shouted again.

Mamishu nudged me gently toward the man as she clung tightly to my hand.

"Halt!" the guard shouted to my mother, pulling our hands apart.

A second guard forced my mother backward, pushing on both of her shoulders as the first man yanked me into his bulky, unfamiliar arms. He held me firmly while yet another guard began pricking the soft white underside of my left forearm with a thick needle. I know I shouldn't have cried, but my skin felt like it was being seared with matches. It burned so badly, I couldn't stop the tears. As he worked, the guard wiped away the blood and daubed the wounds with blue ink, forcing the ink into the holes. He was tattooing a series of crudely shaped numbers into my skin, branding me forever.

I howled and screamed as "B-1148" was inked on my arm. To the SS, I wasn't Michael. I was just a code number ready to be grouped and sorted. I was not the only person to come through Auschwitz and receive the number 1148. As soon as the tattoo numbers reached 20,000, the numbers were recycled with a new letter as a prefix. It helped the SS hide the depth and breadth of their carnage.

After I was tattooed, the guards shaved my head until my scalp was clean and bald. My grandmother and mother watched wordlessly. They had no choice.

Mamishu no doubt wanted to scream and attack my tormentors as my soft blond curls fell to the floor. She knew she would miss the feeling of my wispy locks against her lips as she kissed the top of my head at night.

I kicked and fussed so much that the straight razor nicked my scalp. Mamishu and Bobeshi both winced as a thin trail of blood streaked down over my eyes and onto my lips. But they knew that if they did anything more than flinch, we would all be executed. Auschwitz was clearly not a place for taking stands. Watching her youngest child be tormented like this made Mamishu think of her older son. Was Samuel enduring this same cruelty on the men's side of camp?

Samuel's rock!

Mamishu later told me she suddenly remembered she had left the gray rock Samuel gave her in the pocket of her discarded skirt. Here she was, with a diamond ring hidden under her tongue that she wished she had spit out in order to hide the rock Samuel had given her instead. Her heart ached for the child she couldn't see, and it broke for the child being brutalized in front of her.

"I am an idiot, an idiot!" Mamishu whispered in Bobeshi's ear as she explained.

"*Sha, sha,*" Bobeshi whispered back. "Israel will take care of your boy. Strong. Be strong!"

As punishment for my tantrum, one guard was now holding me down on the dirty floor with his knee pressed into my stomach. Another pressed a foot on my forehead, pinning my head against the ground so that I was immobilized. The more I screamed, the harder the guards pressed down on my body, and I learned in that painful moment that crying wouldn't help anything at this new place. I stayed plenty quiet after that. It was an opening-day lesson that helped save my life.

The same German who cut my hair snipped Mamishu's locks short and shaved the rest clean, while a prisoner— probably a fellow Jew with haircutting experience— unapologetically did the same to Bobeshi. Under different circumstances, I might have laughed at the three of us standing there bald-headed as babies, but I'm certain the sight of my beloved mother and grandmother without hair was upsetting.

While we stood in line that day at Auschwitz, soldiers filed paperwork on us. They kept track of every arrival: name, age, history, and date of death. These records would one day serve as a monumental testament to evil. But on this day the SS remained proud of its efficient camps and its murderous system. My record, which included the number newly inked on my arm, was filed and stored with perfect precision.

What I didn't know then was that my number, B-1148, was one of the last ever tattooed on a prisoner inside Auschwitz. The SS had begun fearing that the Nazi government was losing its footing in the war. They worried the

steadily advancing Soviet army could invade at any time.
Within days of my arrival, they sped up their extermination process and didn't take the time to assign numbers or
bunks. Most prisoners who arrived after my family were
taken straight to the killing chambers. So at Auschwitz,
we were among the lucky ones: chosen to live—at least for
the day.

14

PUNISHMENT AT AUSCHWITZ

"Nein! Gehen sie nicht zusammen!" a guard shouted at me. It sounded similar to Yiddish (*Nit! ir ton nit geyn tsuzamen*), but I really hoped I was misunderstanding. It sounded like the guard was telling me I would not be going with Mamishu and Bobeshi.

He came closer and ripped my fingers from my mother's hand. *"Geh!"* he shouted, pushing me in another direction.

I was separated from my mother and grandmother immediately after the paperwork was complete at Auschwitz. I'm glad I don't remember my walk to the children's bunk. For me, the details have been learned from fellow survivors' accounts.

Had I been at the main camp, I would have passed a building where, each day, about a dozen prisoners were standing with their noses pressed to the brick wall. They never moved.

Those were the prisoners who were pulled from roll call earlier the same day. Their offenses ranged from missing a button on their uniform to tripping during the march toward lineup.

The SS had no tolerance for disorder.

For instance, prisoners were only issued new underwear once every few weeks, and when the SS ranking official Oswald Pohl heard that Jews were murmuring complaints about this, he said that prisoners should be taught "by flogging if necessary" how to take care of their things.

The prisoners who waited nose-to-the-wall, though, weren't waiting to be flogged. They were waiting to be executed. Public shootings happened daily, sending a warning to all prisoners: *Follow orders!* The condemned would wait there for hours, knowing that by the end of the day they would be dead.

It was a better fate than prisoners reassigned to Block 11, however. That was sort of a prison inside the prison. Down below Block 11 lay a basement of horrors, a torture cell. What happened in the courtyard outside that block was also unspeakable. I can't write about what happened there. I'll just say that death was the best possible outcome in Block 11.

One thing I do remember is the sight of smoke rising

from the chimneys of the crematoria at Birkenau. Smoke blew in all directions, day and night.

Auschwitz was like a city with living quarters and work zones that spanned more than forty square kilometers and housed more than a hundred thousand prisoners.

In my section of the fenced-off world, each day condemned women would line up in long columns, stripped naked and forced to stand outside. There, they would wait for the doors to open so they could file in for "showers." There were rumors across camp that those showers were really death chambers, so the SS soldiers took great steps to keep prisoners calm. As women filed in, soldiers called out, "Find a numbered hook and hang your garments. Don't forget your number. You'll be back soon to retrieve your uniforms." Most prisoners weren't fooled. Once the doors closed to the chamber, a deadly poison gas called Zyklon B, which interfered with the breathing process, spilled from the vents. Within minutes, those trapped inside began vomiting and gasping for air until everyone had suffocated.

Each gas chamber was connected to a crematorium—an oven to burn the bodies. The SS used a specially chosen group of Jewish prisoners they called *Sonderkommandos* (special commandos) to drag the bodies from the gas chambers into the ovens. No job was less coveted.

The chimneys at Auschwitz-Birkenau were constantly belching foul smoke, breathing out the souls of Jewish innocents and sending them up to the heavens. Meanwhile, down on earth there was only hell. The humiliation was its own category of torment. Take the bathhouse, for instance. It housed long narrow slabs of stone, like a hollow stone bench that stretched for days. The slabs had hundreds of round holes chiseled out, just inches apart. Those were "toilet seats" where hundreds of prisoners had to sit, skin touching skin, with just seconds to relieve themselves before the next shift of prisoners would sit down.

Prisoners assigned to clean the bathhouse, the *Scheisskommandos* (shit commanders), actually held coveted jobs. They had access to running water all day and weren't at risk of intestinal backup, given their access to toilets. They were also able to hide children inside those holes. Yes, children hid there.

In addition to the torture by contamination, there were whipping stones set randomly about the camps. If a prisoner worked too slowly or dared beg for a break—he would be laid over the stone and whipped on his bare skin seventy-five times. *"Eins! Zwei! Drei!"* Prisoners were forced to count the strokes aloud, in German. If they missed a number, the counting and the whipping would start all over again.

It's miraculous that I was assigned to a children's bunk and spared the deadly alternatives across Auschwitz's city of suffering. I didn't have to stand from three until seven in the morning for roll call in the cold. Mamishu and Bobeshi had to do that. Nazis were obsessed with counting. Sometimes prisoners were counted three times a day. And sometimes, to add to the torture, prisoners had to squat through the entire process. If they lost their balance and fell over, they were whipped.

On the men's side of camp, Papa and Samuel were no doubt enduring much of the same. If anyone was missing at roll call, the entire group would be punished with beatings. That posed a real problem, because every night at least one or two prisoners died of starvation in the bunks. Not even death was a suitable excuse for missing roll call. Prisoners would drag dead bodies along to roll call all the time, just so the rest of the group wouldn't be punished. Prisoners weren't dead and gone until the Nazis made it official.

In the children's bunk, morning roll calls were more humane and there wasn't sunup-to-sundown labor. For the children admitted into Auschwitz, the greatest cruelty was heartbreak. After my arrival processing on that July evening in 1944, I was sent to sleep inside a hot, crowded, dirty barracks where rats nipped at children's toes as they slept, wondering if I would ever see my mother, father, big brother, or grandmother again.

At four years old, I was the youngest child in the bunk. Some of the older boys quickly shared a warning: "Listen, if a German guard comes in here and asks who wants to see his mami or his papa, do not raise your hand. Do you understand?"

Of course I couldn't understand that.

The SS occasionally visited the barracks to "select" children in this manner—but it was a trick. Those who raised their hands were never taken to see their parents. Instead, they were brought to a lab for experimentation. A doctor at the camp named Josef Mengele conducted horrible experiments on children. He called himself "Uncle Mengele" and gave them sweets, but then he used the children like lab animals. They were injected with poisons or underwent operations that left them disfigured, disabled, or dead. Mengele preferred to experiment on twins, but when pairs weren't available, single children would suffice. Much of his work focused on finding the science to create a "perfect race" of people called Aryans. He shared Hitler's view that blond-haired, blue-eyed people were the Aryan ideal.

"Don't raise your hand! Don't raise your hand! Your mother is probably dead by now, anyway!" the older children warned me.

I'm not sure I could have kept my hand down if someone

had promised me he would bring me to my mother. Thankfully, I was never tested.

The bunks were filthy places where the beds were simply wooden shelves tacked to a wall, three in a column. The mattress was just a thin bunch of straw with a piece of cloth over the top, and at least three children slept in each bedshelf at a time. If you had to go to the bathroom at night—well, you just didn't. It was too terrifying to go outside the barracks to the bathhouse alone.

Some children were mortified when they woke up and realized they'd soiled the bed with a bad case of diarrhea. It's just the opposite of what you'd expect: you might think that if you aren't eating much, you don't need to go to the bathroom much. But starvation destroys your intestinal system and leaves you with a messy and embarrassing consequence called "hunger diarrhea." When we could get up in time at night, we ran to a bucket at the back of the room and used it as a toilet. Humiliating.

The older children looked out for me when they could, but they were also human and hungry and just children themselves. I don't think anyone could blame them for stealing some of my food rations each day.

A *blokova* (a woman prisoner in charge of other prisoners) was assigned to bring us food three times a day. We got small pieces of bread, a little scoop of margarine, and a bowl of gray soup. I won't begin to guess what was in that soup. It was disgusting, but it was sustenance. It kept us alive.

The first time I tried the gray soup, some of the nicer big kids warned me to hold my nose while I drank it down. If I couldn't smell it, I was less likely to throw up. There weren't enough bowls or spoons for everyone, so we shared—everyone taking three spoonfuls at a time and then passing the bowl until it was gone. Sometimes hungry children would skip over me or take my turn at the bowl. Other times they stole portions of my bread. If the *blokova* was watching, she intervened. Adults at the camp always protected the children when they could. But as soon as the *blokova* turned her back, someone always seemed to raid my food.

Amid the desperation at Auschwitz were a few bright spots. There was a kind Jewish prisoner who was assigned to babysit us during the day. He would draw pictures and words in the dust on the floor and tell stories to keep us entertained. Our bodies were languishing, but he made sure our minds were not. If he was caught teaching at the camp, he would have been killed, for sure. The older boys took turns standing guard outside the barracks. If an SS soldier came near, we were quickly warned and we formed a circle pretending to play with the pebbles and caterpillars that were our "toys" at the camp.

I don't know how long I could have survived in the camp on the meager rations I was left to consume, had there not been a shocking visitor to the children's bunk one evening.

Maybe it was one week after I arrived or maybe four. I just don't know. The door opened at the front of the long, narrow room and in walked Mamishu!

"Mami is dah, meyn libling!" she shouted in Yiddish. Mami is here, my love! And she ran to me at the back of the room. I was so much smaller than the other boys that I was easy to pick out in the crowd. "Darling, Michael!" She hugged me tight in an embrace that made us both almost whole again.

She was scared by my appearance. In however much time had passed, I had already lost weight. She used her hand to hold open the pocket of her uniform dress so that I could peek inside. *Bread!* Mamishu brought me a whole slice. She didn't pull it out all at once, fearful that someone might steal it. Instead, she discreetly pulled little corners off the bread while it was still in her pocket and she hand-fed me piece after piece while we stood at the back of the barracks, relishing the moment.

My mother couldn't stay long. It wasn't safe. She didn't

know how she could leave me there alone in a bunk with much older children, rats finding their way into the barracks for the night, and no one to even kiss me goodnight at bedtime. But she couldn't stay. If she went missing, her entire bunk of women would be whipped and beaten at roll call, and she would eventually be found.

We said goodbye, but that was not the last time my mother came to visit me in the children's bunk. Once she knew for certain where I was living, she found her way back again and again—always bringing pocketfuls of food, even though she, too, was starving.

One night a *blokova* assigned to monitor our bunk began clubbing my mother over the head with a stick, shooing her out of the room. Fear will cause you to do wild things, and the Jewish guard knew that if my mother was caught in the children's barracks, *she* would be held accountable.

"*Nit!*" my mother shouted at the *blokova*. "You will *not* keep me from my son!" My petite mother, not quite five feet tall and weak from starvation, held the *blokova* off, pushing her back with all of her strength until the female guard relented.

That scene played out regularly. Mamishu gained scars on her head, not from clubbings at roll call but from scrabbles with female prisoners guarding the children's bunk.

Her visits were a blessing—but sometimes a curse, too.

On nights when she couldn't make it to me because her workshift ran too long, I assumed she had been killed, just like so many of the other boys' mothers. I cried silently, crammed between other starving children in a bed made of wood and straw.

On those nights, Mamishu also went to sleep anxious and fearful. She imagined she could hear my stomach moaning with hunger, and it hurt her heart to know she wouldn't have the chance to bring me food again for twenty-four more hours.

Finally, fear overcame her. She panicked, believing I would die soon if she didn't do something drastic. She devised a plan and talked it over with Bobeshi. Always cautious, Bobeshi was hesitant.

"Sophie, you could be killed. Michael could be killed. The whole bunk—everyone would be in jeopardy," Bobeshi whispered as they talked in hushed voices in bed.

"We could all be killed at any moment if it is the SS guards' will!" Mamishu said softly but firmly.

Bobeshi knew her daughter-in-law was right.

15

NEWS FROM THE FENCE

Mamishu was hardly the only prisoner in her barracks who was a mother of small children, but she might have been one of the few whose children were still alive. She hoped her bunkmates would sympathize with her.

"My son Michael can't survive alone any longer in the children's bunk," she declared one evening as her bunkmates were all using the last of their daily energy to climb onto high wooden beds. "He has no protector. Some of the older boys are stealing his food, and it's only a matter of time before he dies of starvation," Mamishu told them.

"I've lost four children, my husband, and my parents. What do you expect any of us to do about it?" asked one woman.

Bobeshi tried to help. "She's not asking you to do anything. Just the opposite—she's asking you not to say a word."

"I'm bringing Michael here to hide in our barracks," Mamishu announced, waiting for protest, as she imagined there would be mass opposition to hiding a child there.

She needn't have worried so much. There was almost an unspoken rule among the women at Auschwitz—if you see a child, you protect him. Women assigned to gardening duties would steal vegetables from those they harvested. They kept some for themselves, of course, but they regularly sought out children in camp who desperately needed the nutrients.

The precious items prisoners surrendered when they arrived at Auschwitz were brought to a warehouse facility known as Kanada, the German spelling of a country that symbolized wealth to the inmates of the concentration camp. Prisoners known as *Kommandos* worked at the Kanada facility, sorting items and preparing them for shipment back to Germany. Women at Kanada stole underwear and sweaters for children, even though the penalty for anyone caught stealing was death.

Women who worked in the tailoring shop would covertly turn sheets and blankets into small jackets and undergarments. Then, like Mamishu, they would sneak into the children's bunk somehow to distribute them.

Compared with the Jewish prisoners, some Christian

prisoners at the camp had slightly more access. They, too, used their positions to help children at the camp. They never cared if the children were Jewish or not.

So the huge crowd of women who shared a bunk with Mamishu and Bobeshi at Auschwitz all easily agreed they would keep me hidden, if my mother could sneak me into the barracks. I don't know how many women there were—probably more than six hundred sleeping and eating in one room with only about 160 beds to divide among them. No one argued.

Mamishu didn't tell me her plan in advance. She worried she would fail to find the right opportunity to sneak me to her barracks. But one night when she visited me late, she whispered very quietly in my ear so that no one else could possibly hear.

"Michael, we are going."

"What?" I could not believe it. I'm sure I must have thought we were escaping Auschwitz, but being anywhere with my mother and grandmother at that age was better than anywhere on earth without them.

It was risky for me to sneak across the camp with my mother. Children rarely ventured outside one small area, so if a guard had seen my little figure scampering toward the adult quarters, he might have stopped us.

We did it somehow. Mamishu snuck me from my barracks

to hers without any SS patrol on the ground or up in watch-towers spotting anything suspicious. Maybe they thought she was assigned to watch the children and was taking me to the bathhouse? I don't know how she did it, but when we rushed in the door of her barracks, everyone inside greeted me warmly. Even the two "elders" assigned to the bunk nodded in my direction. Those were the prisoners who managed the bar-racks, doling out food and making sure rules were followed.

When the crowd parted, I saw my frail-looking Bobeshi sitting on the edge of a bed with her arms outstretched, waiting for me to fall into her embrace.

"Michael!" She kissed my cheeks on both sides and then frowned at my gaunt appearance. She was never much for buoyant greetings, but my grandmother was clearly thrilled to see me. She told me she had missed me and that she saved a place in the bed just for her *zeisele.*

That night, Bobeshi held me very close when I tucked myself between my mother and grandmother in the wooden bed-shelf. It had been getting cold at night, so the tight squeeze kept us warm. Without much body fat, it was hard not to be cold as autumn fell in Poland.

Very early in the morning, before the sun came up, the women woke and the bunk elders passed around small cups, half-filled with artificial coffee. That was breakfast. My mother let me sip from her cup, but it tasted disgusting.

She promised me soup at lunchtime and then told me she had to go stand for roll call.

"You will lie right here, my darling. She pushed back the pile of straw on the bed and had me lie flat on the wooden board. Then she covered me with straw and said, "There, darling. Stay very still and if you are a good boy and are very quiet, I'll be back at lunchtime with food." Then she warned me, "If someone enters the bunk while I am gone, you are not to move a muscle or say a word. Do your very best hiding!"

I promised her I would.

Now that my mother had solved one problem she was squarely focused on her other great concern. She couldn't stop wondering if Papa was able to care for Samuel on the men's side of camp. She was desperate to know if they were both safe.

She wondered if barbarians had shaved Samuel's hair like mine and if she would recognize him the next time she saw him. She wondered if he cried at night. She didn't dare imagine his death, though. That possibility was too painful to even consider.

It was common knowledge that if you wanted to get news from the men's side of camp, you had to find your way to the electrified fence that separated the men from the women.

There, prisoners traded information in whispers and cries through the dangerous metal fencing.

Once again, my mother was best suited to do the sneaking around. Bobeshi worked in the Kanada warehouse, sorting and piling. It was one of the few jobs she could manage easily, given her age. Plus, the bunk counted on Bobeshi to help "organize."

At Auschwitz, prisoners "organized" to meet needs in the barracks. If spoons were in short supply (which they always were), Bobeshi could organize some from suitcases in the Kanada warehouse. If socks were in demand, Bobeshi tucked some in her uniform dress pocket. She'd be killed if she was caught, but she knew which guards generously looked the other way.

So it was Mamishu, who at roll call, would seek out a job near the electrified fence. She managed to secure an assignment carrying bricks that were being used to build a structure in just the right location in the camp. It was a terrible chore in her weakened condition, and the job would prove difficult. But the exhaustion was worth the price of an update on Samuel and Papa. Maybe she could even catch a glimpse of them!

When she arrived at the worksite, she immediately noticed a group of men working quietly on the other side of the fence. One of them caught sight of her, too, and gave a veiled nod.

"An die Arbeit!" the guards shouted on my mother's side of the fence. Get to work!

Hours passed before her SS guards finally took a break, stopping to eat and to make small talk under the shade of an oak tree while the prisoners continued to work, unattended.

Out of sight of the guards, Mamishu ran to the electrified barrier. She motioned for the men to come near. "Israel and Samuel Bornstein!" she said quickly. "A father and son from Żarki, Poland. Israel is average height with thick, brown, curly—"

One worker cut her off. "I'd say we all have about the same haircut," he said as he touched his shaved head.

Mamishu had no time for humor. "Samuel is just a boy. He's about this tall." She touched her chin and continued. "Samuel and Israel Bornstein—please, do you have any idea if they're safe?"

The men didn't seem to recognize the names but promised to return by the end of the workday with some information. They said if they could, they would even bring Samuel to the fence.

Each load of bricks Mamishu carried that afternoon seemed to grow heavier without growing larger. She was worn and worried. When the gray soup made of rutabaga, potato, and buckwheat had been doled out in the barracks at midday, she had given her portion to me.

Late in the day the guards took another break. Just as the sun was beginning to set, Mamishu noticed the group of men she had seen earlier nervously approach the fence again. She didn't know if they appeared anxious because they weren't supposed to be there, or if they were anxious to tell her something.

Samuel and my father weren't with them.

"I guess your name is Sophie," one man whispered through the diamond-shaped cutouts in the fence. "Sophie, I'm so sorry. Israel and your son are gone. They were taken to the killing chambers."

Mamishu fell to the ground. She later told me that her heart literally felt like it had been gouged from her chest with an ax. She tried to remember Samuel's face, but all she could picture was the rock he had given her the day we arrived at Auschwitz—the little round, smooth rock! Why had she tossed her skirt in the pile without saving that precious gift?

She lay in a heap, knees and face in the dirt by the fence, and decided it was time to give up. She had had enough of hunger and loss and fear. If she'd had the energy in that instant, she might have leaped against the electric fence and ended her life, as many other prisoners had done. Instead, she waited there for SS guards to find her and put a bullet in her head for abandoning her work detail.

Minutes passed. The men who had shared the awful news disappeared because they had no choice. It was time for them to line up and be counted again. The women working near her didn't seem to notice she was there in a heap on the ground. Or if they did notice, they didn't care to waste their energy trying to save her. The guards were still distracted.

But then Mamishu thought of me. She knew I might not last one week in Auschwitz without her protection. She used the last of her strength to put her despair aside. She would return to it some other day, but right now she had one son left and she was determined to keep me safe. Mamishu heaved her limp body off the ground and, after roll call, returned to the women's bunk, where I lay napping in secret under the straw mattress.

16

AN UNEXPECTED DEPARTURE

The Nazis were nothing if not efficient. They made use of as many healthy Jewish prisoners as possible, scouring their concentration camps often to round up the best workers for particular jobs.

One day at roll call, a group of officers in sharp uniforms appeared and demanded that every woman in my mother's unit run laps around an enclosed ring, like horses being put through their paces at a show. The women had to strip naked first. The SS wanted to see how much fat the women had left on their bodies. Women so skinny their bones jutted out in all directions wouldn't do. They wanted to pick the healthiest women—and the process had the added benefit of completely humiliating the prisoners.

My mother, like all of the other undernourished women at the camp, tired quickly but was determined not to reveal her fatigue. She ignored the sharp pains on the bottom of her toes every time she set a foot down. She had horrible festering blisters yet didn't dare complain. Even something like blisters on your feet could get you labeled "unfit to work," a guaranteed death sentence.

Every time Mamishu passed the officers she inhaled to hide her loud panting. Bobeshi tried to do the same but was unsuccessful. In very short order, her sprinting turned to jogging and her jogging turned to walking.

The women were allowed to dress. Then ten women were picked from the crowd; my mother was one of them. The chosen few were then interrogated.

"What skills do you have? What experience?"

"Oh, I can expertly pack ammunition," Mamishu boasted. She told them of her work at Pionki.

From her experience, Mamishu knew that packing ammunition required much less physical labor than most of the work at Auschwitz. She hoped she could be reassigned to similar work.

"Look at my tiny fingers," she said, holding up her petite hands. "Perfect for bullet packing!" she trilled in broken German. "My mother-in-law—she's just over there—is a real expert, too!"

The men weren't interested in Bobeshi, though.

"What's your number?" they barked at my mother.

Mamishu pulled up her sleeve and displayed her tattoo. One officer wrote her ID down on paper, and in that moment my mother's fate was sealed.

"You have fifteen minutes to clean yourself up and report to the front gates. You will be leaving Auschwitz."

Mamishu was being sent away to a labor camp in Austria. For other women, this would have been welcome news. But Mamishu felt like she had just walked into a trap. She thought about protesting, but what would she say? *My son is here, hiding away in the shadows. He'll die if I'm not here to protect him. I can't leave!* No, there was nothing my mother could do or say.

Mamishu raced to the bunk where I was hiding. She rustled the straw mattress and panicked when she saw I wasn't there.

At that moment, I giggled from behind a wooden crate in the corner of the room. Sometimes I would move from hiding place to hiding place for a change of scenery during the day, and I was happy to see Mamishu appear in the middle of the afternoon.

She didn't look happy at all.

"Michael, I have to go, my darling," she told me as tears streamed down her face. "I promise, I will see you again someday, *zeisele*. We'll be free and I will find you. But right now, I have no choice. I have to leave you for a little while."

She offered no specifics about when we would be reunited. She only promised that Grandma Dora would keep me safe and make sure I had enough to eat and drink.

"Tell Bobeshi that I love her," Mamishu said. "You two take care of one another."

I wanted to cry, but I was careful to keep my own promise at Auschwitz. I said nothing. I just kissed my Mamishu on the cheek and crawled under my pile of straw as she left. I packed an extra handful of straw over my toes and a handful over my face, then waited quietly for my grandmother's return. Heartbreak was starting to feel as natural as hunger and fear to me. I was numb with hurt.

17

A LUCKY ILLNESS

In the weeks that followed, there were drastic changes at the death camp. When we had first arrived, soldiers were efficiently killing thousands of prisoners each day. Roll call was endless but orderly. Work routines were brutal but organized.

Suddenly, though, the system at Auschwitz seemed to break down and things got chaotic. Watchtowers went unmanned, there weren't enough guards to supervise every work assignment, and the number of SS men seemed to diminish by the day.

There were rumors that Allied forces, including the armies of the United States and Soviet Union, had gained the upper hand in the war. We often heard bombing and heavy artillery fire in the distance, and it gave every prisoner hope that freedom was coming.

As the Germans realized they were losing ground, the SS soldiers' primary focus turned to hiding evidence of their crimes. They didn't want anyone to know the evils committed inside extermination camps like Auschwitz. They needed to clear the prisoners out of Auschwitz fast—even faster than those fake showers and massive ovens would allow.

On January 17, 1945, Grandma Dora woke up in the middle of the night to the sound of me moaning. My skin was burning hot, and sweat ran from my pores. There was no water in our bunk. There was no medicine, of course. Bobeshi was helpless to bring down my fever.

She jumped off the bed-shelf where we had been sleeping and ran to the window, which was shut tight to keep out the cold. She couldn't open the glass—the cold air would have woken all the women inside the bunk and left them freezing. Instead, she pressed her hands against the ice-cold panes until she could no longer feel her fingers. Then she ran back to my side and held her palms against my forehead. She did this over and over, turning her hands into virtual ice packs to cool my fever.

"What are you doing?" our Hungarian shelf-mate whispered as Bobeshi returned again and again to my side.

"Never mind, Alida. Go back to sleep," Bobeshi said.

She did not want to scare our neighbors, but she knew that whatever I had was quite serious. Honestly, even a small cold could be perilous at Auschwitz, where malnourished bodies were too weak to fight off invaders of any size.

Fortunately, Alida didn't need any more coaxing. She was snoring again within seconds. Grandma Dora needed a little time to decide her next move. There was no roll call and there were no formal job assignments most days now. Auschwitz was in disarray, but Bobeshi had heard that the infirmary was still in operation.

I know—how ironic that a camp designed for death would have an infirmary, a small hospital supposedly used to protect prisoners' health. The Germans had violated every rule in the book, of course, but they didn't want the rest of the world to know that. So each death camp had a working infirmary.

"Michael, I know you are weak, my *bubeleh*—darling," Grandma Dora whispered as sun started pouring in through the windows. "We are going to stand up now, and you can't say a word. Just hold my hand and walk. When I stop, you stop."

I was so tired. Walking—even standing—seemed impossible.

Grandma Dora lifted me off the straw, which was moist with my sweat. She carried me to the door and set me down on my little bare feet. She helped me slip into the wooden shoes I was given on my first day at Auschwitz. They had been so big on me then, but even with so little food a four-year-old body still wants to grow. Those shoes practically fit me now.

"Where are we going, Bobeshi?" I asked.

Grandma Dora put her index finger to her lips to remind me not to speak. Fortunately, the infirmary was only a few hundred yards away from our block. Bobeshi hurried me through the camp, ducking behind structures whenever we could. Luckily, there was so little order at the camp now that most remaining guards were still sleeping. Artillery fire in the far-off distance was the only sound of life. It was Allied forces, nearing the camp.

When we arrived along the side of the infirmary, Bobeshi tried to peer in through one of the windows, but it was too high.

"Come here, Michael," she whispered, pulling me toward her.

Bobeshi strained to lift me onto her shoulders.

My eyes could just peer over the window's ledge. The cold air had temporarily given me a jolt of life, and I was eager to help.

"What do you see?" she asked.

"There are *eins, zwei, drei, vier, funf* women sleeping," I counted in my newly learned German. "I don't see any soldiers, Bobeshi." And by some strange sort of luck, I was right!

No guards were manning the front of the infirmary either. We slipped inside, found two empty beds, and—once our hearts stopped racing from fear—fell fast asleep.

Maybe hours passed. I don't know for sure. But eventually I awoke to Grandma Dora standing over me, along with a doctor. He was German and wore a Nazi uniform. But you could tell from his expression he was kind. He told me I was very sick and I would be staying in the infirmary for at least five days—unless I died first. Bobeshi would be allowed to stay with me because she had been exposed to my germs. The SS tried to avoid letting disease ravage its supply of workers.

The camp, he told Bobeshi, might be evacuated soon. He had learned that prisoners would be marching out of the fencing shortly. "You'll be safe here, though," he told my grandmother.

I couldn't believe I was allowed to sleep in my own bed in the infirmary. It had soft padding above the wood plank, and even though the sheets were dirty and stained, they were sheets! I had sheets! This was a definite improvement from life in the bunk.

The few doctors and nurses left to man the infirmary were nice. They didn't seem anything like the SS soldiers who marched right outside the doors, even if they held the same high rank. There had been evil doctors at work in that building, like Josef Mengele, the torturer who experimented on children. But Mengele had disappeared along with many other high-ranking officers in camp.

The next evening, Bobeshi and I went to sleep with resolved strength to survive. We awoke to the sound of chaos. It was January 18, 1945, and soldiers were shouting commands at the top of their lungs. They blew whistles. Boots marched. Whips cracked. Gunshots sounded. It was pandemonium right outside the window.

I climbed into Grandma Dora's bed, and we both hid under the sheets because we didn't know what else to do. Some patients near us in the infirmary jumped up and ran out to rejoin their bunkmates. They feared that anyone left behind would be executed. Bobeshi chose to trust the doctor we had met the day earlier. He had told us we would be safe there, so we stayed.

The chaos continued for hours. Bobeshi allowed herself to peek just once out the window; she saw Alida and Belka and our entire bunk lined up in the cold with no coats.

Finally, the noise started moving farther and farther away. Then a strange quiet came over the camp.

We later learned that sixty thousand prisoners were marched out of Auschwitz toward the town of Wodzisław

Śląski. It was a trip that would take days on foot through rough forest terrain; tens of thousands died along the way. They were shot for moving too slow, or simply died from starvation and exposure. It was a journey that was dubbed the "Death March."

We would have died, my grandmother and I. We could never have survived the march—a young child and an old woman. Even those who made it to Wodzisław Śląski were then loaded onto a freight train bound for concentration camps in Germany, like Buchenwald and Dachau.

I would like to be able to tell you exactly what illness saved my life. My condition is described in a handwritten list of Auschwitz inmates now preserved at Yad Vashem Holocaust Remembrance Center in Israel. The first archivist who translated the document believed I was being treated for diphtheria, a potentially deadly infection. But two other translators see the Latin medical term "dystrophie," a condition that simply means I was "wasting away."

The name doesn't really matter. That piece of paper recovered by a museum years after the war made one miracle clear. Sickness saved my life. Over the next few days, SS guards would periodically return to the camp on motorcycles and in trucks. They carried machine guns and searched barracks for any prisoners left behind. Anyone they found, they shot on sight. I later learned that some survivors outside the infirmary managed to hide themselves by tucking into a pile of dead bodies. The returning Nazi soldiers never searched the infirmary though. Maybe they were afraid of the germs. Maybe we just weren't meant to die.

All I know is, my grandmother and I had managed to escape another road that led to death by the bizarre and timely grace of an illness.

Nine days later, with no SS guards in sight, Soviet troops marched through the gates of Auschwitz as light snow fell under the sign that carried the disgusting lie about work making us free.

Of the hundreds of thousands of children who had been delivered by train to Auschwitz, only fifty-two under the age of eight survived. They were the world's best hiders. I was one of them.

When soldiers in their rugged uniforms, caps, and bulging leather satchels reached us, we knew we didn't need to fear them because they were smiling at us. The Soviet soldiers who came to liberate us brought chocolates and cookies. We showed them our tattoos to identify ourselves, but they pushed our arms aside and asked for our names. We weren't prisoners anymore—we were survivors. We weren't numbers anymore—we were people. And we were free.

"I am Michael," I told the soldiers.

18

VISITORS FOR RUTH

The orphanage in Częstochowa had become a beehive of activity in the late winter of 1944–45. The grounds were filled with children who were orphaned during the war. Inside, dozens of children studied science and religion in class or prayed at mass in the chapel. On the outdoor playground, girls dressed in hand-me-down wool swing coats played *klasy*, a game similar to hopscotch, and boys drew pictures with sticks in the dirt and chased one another. Their laughter filled the spaces where now-vanished SS soldiers had once shouted in the halls.

The city had officially been liberated by Russian troops, and only ten days earlier a visitor had arrived at the front steps of the convent. She was a tall, slender woman with long golden hair that fell to the middle of her back. She was invited into the Mother Superior's office, where she explained that she hoped to adopt a child.

The woman had come from Switzerland, and for many years she and her husband had hoped to become parents. She began to cry as she explained it must not have been in God's plan. But then she read news reports of the many children who had been orphaned here in Poland after their parents were killed at the hands of the SS, and her heart had pulled her to this church.

The Mother Superior spent a long time speaking with this woman and found her to be sincere and honest in her desire to adopt. She brought the woman to the orphanage playground and told her that every child there needed a home.

The nun warned her, though, that the orphanage had a very strict rule. No child would be forced into an adoption. If a boy or girl wanted to leave with a family, they could. If they wanted to stay, the church would never turn its back on them. There were no exceptions to the rule.

After the woman watched and visited with the boys and girls at the orphanage for many hours, her eyes kept returning to one little girl with olive skin so warm it looked as though she had been basking in sunlight. There was little sunshine in the child's smile, though. The hopeful mother-to-be decided if she could only bring this girl home, she could help her find the sunlight within and they could be a family.

The little girl's name was Kristina. She was five years old, and her voice was every bit as lovely as her face. The woman told the Mother Superior she believed God had brought her here to this place for a reason. She belonged with Kristina.

The head nun was elated. Kristina was such a sensitive, kind, and brilliant little girl. She would thrive in a good home, and this woman seemed like an ideal fit. But when the nuns told Kristina that the tall, golden-haired woman would be taking her home to Switzerland, the little girl screamed, "No! I won't go." She ran from the room shouting and wailing, "You're not my mother! I won't leave with this strange woman. Please, I won't go!"

The nuns had never seen Kristina behave like this. She never raised her voice and rarely cried, not even when she first arrived at the orphanage and was clearly terrified. They had thought Kristina would be pleased to have been chosen by a kind family. Nevertheless, the orphanage rule superseded all, and the Mother Superior reluctantly told the woman from Switzerland that Kristina would be staying with her church family.

Only days later, three more visitors appeared outside the grand wooden doors at the front of the church in Częstochowa, asking to speak with the Mother Superior.

A short, dark-haired gentleman with a long thick beard, his wife, and a younger man who said he was the couple's nephew were all led into the nun's quarters. The couple believed that their daughter might have been left outside the building's perimeter during the war and could now be living there at the orphanage. "Her name is Ruth," they told the Mother Superior.

"I'm sorry," the nun said. "There have been many children left at our doorstep over the last six years, but there is no child here named Ruth." The Mother Superior went on to explain the church's rule for mutually agreed-on adoptions.

The three visitors were, of course, Sam and Cecia Jonisch and Ruth's cousin Eli. They had spent two and a half years hiding in a tiny attic at a farmhouse outside Żarki, and as soon as they learned it was safe to walk the streets again, they had only one mission.

Cecia reached in her pocket and pulled out a swatch of white fabric with pink and green flowers. She had known that one day it might be the only proof she had that she was Ruth's mother, so every day they were separated she had attached it with a safety pin to the outside of her slip. Cecia knew that if she was ever captured by the SS and sent to a concentration camp, her undergarments might be the only possession she could keep. Thus the swatch rested on her hip always, just as her baby girl had done long ago.

When she held out the fabric, one look at the Mother Superior's face told Cecia that her daughter was here at the orphanage.

The nun could not conceal her joy. Every article of clothing and personal item a child arrived with at the church was kept in a box for as long as the orphan remained there. Kristina's floral dress had been tucked away for safekeeping.

Cecia could hear her heart beating in her own ears, her body literally shaking with joy and anticipation.

Still, there was a rule. If Kristina felt safe leaving the orphanage with this family, it would be so. But if she did not, the Jonisches could not leave with this child.

The Mother Superior told her excited guests, "Only one visitor at a time. We need to be careful not to overwhelm Kristina. She's a very sensitive girl."

Uncle Sam, still haunted by the image of his daughter left alone on a bench just outside, insisted he should enter first. It had been years since he'd seen her, but Ruth still looked as delicate and lovely as ever. She looked nervous, too. The Mother Superior had told her she believed her parents had returned, but Ruth was scared it was a lie.

"*Zeisele!*" Sam cried. Ruth looked at this short, bearded

man and let out a scream that could shatter eardrums. Sam tried to explain how he and her mother had left her behind to save her. They were Jewish and they had no choice.

This only terrified Ruth more. She could not be Jewish. She loved Jesus and prayed to him with all her heart every single day. Besides, Jews were filthy, horrid pigs. She could not be one of them.

Sam didn't know how to comfort his child. She was too big to scoop up and hold now; she had grown half a foot, and her round cheeks were more angular and mature. No longer a toddler, she was a five-year-old girl. Sam touched his hand to Ruth's back to soothe her, saying her name over and over again.

But she shrieked and pushed his hand away, shouting, "My name is Kristina!"

Cecia, who could hear the outburst from the hall outside, pleaded with the Mother Superior. "Ruth can't possibly remember us. She had just celebrated her third birthday when we had to send her away. But please, please—she is ours. You saw the fabric from her dress. You know she is my child!"

The Mother Superior's heart was torn. When Uncle Sam stepped out of the room, she could barely look him in the face. The nun turned to Cecia and asked her to try. Cecia had never imagined a reunion like this. She never thought that should she find her cherished daughter one day she would be told that she could not keep her. By now, my aunt was wholly skeptical and heartsick.

She rounded the corner into the room where Ruth waited. Cecia was breathless at the sight of her daughter, who sat staring out the window. Ruth's profile looked quite different and yet just exactly the same. Cecia felt a force drawing her to run and embrace her daughter, but she used every bit of restraint inside her body to fight it. She did not want to scare her child more.

Instead, she stood in the doorway of the cream-walled orphanage bedroom and sang. *"Aleph, Bet, Vet. (Aleph, Bet, Vet.) Gimmel, Dalet, Hay. (Gimmel, Dalet, Hay.) . . ."* It was the Hebrew alphabet song; Ruth had loved singing this tune with her mother.

Ruth tilted her head just an inch. She, too, was fighting some powerful force that was willing her to turn away from the window and look at the woman who was singing. She was scared to be disappointed—but she also wanted to look.

Cecia just kept on singing. Moments passed and, suddenly, Ruth spun around. She saw Cecia, and her stonelike demeanor melted into happiness. Smiling and crying at once, she launched herself into her mother's arms. She remembered that song and that embrace and that face. She remembered being loved by this beautiful dark-haired woman.

In that instant, Ruth knew she would never be an orphan again.

19

PICTURE IN HISTORY

I would like to tell you that on the day Soviet soldiers came to free the prisoners from Auschwitz, all of us went home and lived happily ever after. But it wasn't like that at all. People were sick and hungry, and had no means of transportation. Some people's homes had been destroyed, and others came from cities that were still under German rule. Auschwitz was liberated, but the war was not over. Germany had not been defeated; Nazi invaders had not been driven out of every town or country. In most cases, prisoners had no family left. I was lucky to have Bobeshi. And, of course, I was waiting for Mamishu to find me again now that the war was ending.

The first night of freedom we all stayed at the camp, which was now in the control of the Soviets. We slept in the barracks but with pillows! The Soviets let us raid the Kanada warehouse for fresh blankets and clothing, leather shoes and wool coats. Bobeshi found a lavender silk slip, which she wore under a thick white cotton nightdress, and she padded around the barracks in tall leather boots to complete the strangely luxurious ensemble. We were allowed to use the bathhouses to shower and covered ourselves in a special disinfectant to kill any lice. We got fresh water from the kitchen whenever we needed it.

The backdrop hadn't changed. But the mood on the night of liberation was so festive it was almost possible to forget we were in a death camp.

"Bobeshi, is Mamishu coming back here?" I asked.

My grandmother waved her hand at me, urging me not to ask her such a question.

"She said we would be together after the war, Bobeshi!" I persisted.

"Michael, *zeisele*, let's talk another evening. Tonight is for celebrating."

We did celebrate. In every bunkhouse there was dancing and singing. The pots and pans and spoons we coveted like gold in the camp were indulgently being used for drumming. The Soviets shared their vodka with the male prisoners. And people would spontaneously shout, "We are free! We are free! We are free!"

Bobeshi didn't dance, but she let her tan leather boots dangle over the edge of a middle bunk bed, swaying her legs from side to side in time with the makeshift music as she soaked in the scene.

I climbed up next to her. "Bobeshi, what does everyone mean when they say, 'We're free and we're going home'? What's going to happen?"

Bobeshi looked at me in shock. I understand now, of course, why my grandmother was so stunned by my question. Who wouldn't know what "free" means?

I didn't. As Grandma Dora kept swaying her legs to the beat of the spoon-pot-pan drumming, she suddenly roared with crazy laughter. It startled me, I'm sure. I couldn't remember ever seeing Bobeshi laugh. Actually, the sound of laughter had become almost as foreign to me by then as the notion of freedom and home. And the kind of laughter I was hearing now, not just from Bobeshi but from the other survivors as well, was the kind of unbridled laughter that comes in a moment where anger, fear, frustration, hope, and joy are all mixed together—bubbling over like lava.

We were celebrating in a camp where dead bodies were piled ten feet high by Block 11. Our bellies were hollow from starvation and our hearts were broken from loss. I don't know what the grown-ups around me were feeling.

I just enjoyed the music and anxiously dreamed of finding Mamishu.

Grandma Dora was nothing like my mother. Where Mamishu was lighthearted and lively, Bobeshi was more stoic and somber. Seeing her laugh made me feel better instantly about whatever came next.

It made my heart practically burst thinking about seeing Mamishu again. I couldn't wait to let her wrap me up in her arms, and I knew she'd be kissing the top of my head where the hair was beginning to grow back. I was excited to tell her about the big bed I had gotten in the infirmary. She wouldn't believe I'd had it all to myself. I wanted to tell her how the German soldiers had left and then how the good soldiers came and gave me chocolate and cookies.

"Michael," Bobeshi said as we lay in bed that night face-to-face. "You know Mamishu is gone now, the same way your papa and your big brother are not here with us anymore, my *libling*."

"No, she isn't." I said this very matter-of-factly. I knew Mamishu would have told me if she was never coming back. She had specifically promised we would be reunited.

Bobeshi said nothing in response. I guess she didn't have the energy to argue with me.

In the morning, no one had to wake up early for roll call.

The Soviet soldiers shouted through camp that food was available in the Germans' kitchen. Breakfast at a free Auschwitz meant eggs cooked over a stove and buckwheat porridge with cream. There were crackers with two kinds of compote, which had been kept in a special storage room for SS guards.

The Soviet doctors who arrived at camp overnight warned us that if we ate too much too fast, our weakened stomachs wouldn't be able to digest it and we could die from overeating. That scared me.

"This, Michael, tastes like God's greatest craft, doesn't it?" Bobeshi asked me with a grin as we nibbled at crispy crackers like mice.

We were trying really hard to pace ourselves and eat slowly like the doctors had said.

"Would you like another package?" a soldier asked Bobeshi. He saw how she enjoyed the crackers and offered her more.

Bobeshi was shocked. "If you have enough to spare," she said quickly. She thanked the soldier, but when he walked away my grandmother tucked the package deep inside her pocket. She had spent six months "organizing" to survive. She didn't know how to do anything else.

More Soviet soldiers arrived in trucks late in the day.

They were turning Auschwitz into an unofficial "displaced persons camp." It would be a holding ground where prisoners could stay until more permanent housing was available or until people found their way home. The soldiers were working with several Jewish refugee organizations and the International Red Cross to help survivors trace relatives. More permanent camps were being established where homeless survivors could eventually stay for months or even years.

The soldiers asked everyone to fill out paperwork. We waited our turn, but while we stood there in line, I recognized one of the older boys who had been in my first bunk at Auschwitz. He was maybe eight years old and he was sobbing.

"Bobeshi, I know that boy!" I said, pointing. "Why is he crying?" I was too insecure to approach the older boy myself.

"Little one, come here," Grandma Dora said. She coaxed him over. Bobeshi didn't hug him the way Mamishu might have done, or wipe his tears. But with genuine concern she leaned over him and asked, "What is it? What's wrong, child?"

At first, the boy was crying so hard she couldn't understand his answer. Other women gathered around, also hoping to help.

In between sobs the boy explained that he couldn't re-member his last name. He had even forgotten the first names of his mother and father, whom he had known only as Mamishu and Papa.

Just as Bobeshi was reaching out to console him, another woman stepped in.

"Tell me your first name," said the woman, whose face bore red scars that looked like burns.

He told her.

"Well, you'll come with me until we sort it all out. We'll have each other until we find our loved ones, darling."

The scar-faced woman looked at Bobeshi to be sure there was no protest. Bobeshi nodded in approval, and the woman led the boy to a wide wooden table at the front of the room where she would take over his guardianship.

Bobeshi leaned way over to whisper in my ear. "Now, see. Aren't we lucky to have each other, Michael? *Baruch atah Adonai*"—thanks to God—"we are family. And soon, we will be home."

When it was our turn to fill out paperwork, there were military translators there to help. They spoke Polish, Hun-garian, German, and even a tiny bit of Yiddish.

I heard one soldier ask Bobeshi, "Where are the boy's parents?"

As she turned her head to look at me, I glanced away and pretended not to pay attention. I heard her, though.

"Verstorben," she whispered to the soldier. Dead.

My heart pounded. I didn't believe what Bobeshi had said. Mamishu wasn't dead. I felt certain, at that moment anyway, that my mother was coming back from wherever the SS had taken her.

I waited for the man to ask my grandmother for some proof, but he just nodded and scribbled something on our papers.

My heart wouldn't stop thudding. Even when I went to sleep in the newly cleaned barracks that night, I heard a thumping in my ears until I finally fell asleep.

I had a terrible dream that night. I don't remember what it was, but perhaps it was the nightmare that haunted me for years to come: In this dream Mamishu was going into the big building at Auschwitz where so many people lined up to enter—naked, compressed together like one mob of ribs and skin. On the other side, Jewish laborers shoveled out limp, dead bodies as fast as they could. In the dream Mami's corpse went through a big machine that turned her into soap. Then I was in the machine and I was being smashed between giant rollers. All the bones in my face and then in my stomach were shattering into a million tiny fragments, and my skin was melting. I was turning into soap, too.

When I woke up, I was pinned tight under the arms of my grandmother, who was holding me down so I would stop flailing.

"*Sha, sha*, Michael. You are safe. You are safe. You are safe. I won't leave you, my *libling*. You are safe. You are safe."

I finally stopped crying and fell back into a deep, dreamless slumber.

On our second morning of freedom, sunlight flooded in through the window of our bunk. Bobeshi and I dressed in the clean clothes we'd acquired from the Kanada warehouse. I had a new pair of shoes to wear. I mean, they weren't really new—but they weren't the oversized wooden clogs I'd first been issued. The worn leather on this pair felt soft on my callused feet.

Once again, the morning brought a relative feast of foods.

"Ladies and gentlemen, please heed the doctors' warnings and take care when you eat. There will be provisions available throughout the day." *Ladies. Gentlemen. Please.* There were so many words that were foreign to me in any language. I had never heard soldiers speak so kindly to Jews.

The breakfast that morning was among the most beautiful sights I have ever seen. There was a table where hundreds of hardboiled eggs filled a clean metal serving tray. There were golden brown biscuits and burgundy beets. It was a rainbow of food. I was amazed at the feel of warm food in my belly. Warm food, what an amazing comfort! And Mamishu would have loved the beets because she always—

Oh, Mamishu. I missed her so.

I pushed my plate back a few inches because suddenly just the smell of these new foods was making my belly do flips.

"Eat, *zeisele*," Grandma Dora urged. She touched my forehead to make sure my fever hadn't returned. I had seemingly beaten my illness. She was still worried about me, though.

"I'm not sick, Bobeshi," I said. "I want Mamishu."

My grandmother just patted my hand and looked away.

Days went by. Most of the snow that fell the day we were liberated had melted, leaving the camp a slushy mess. It all seemed so much cleaner now, though. The chimneys were no longer belching out that evil, ash-filled smoke. Our clothes were clean and our blankets had been rid of lice.

Bobeshi kept telling me, "We're going home soon—very soon."

I didn't remember anything about Żarki, but I imagine I was thinking Mamishu was already there waiting for me.

Three or four more days passed, and then one morning the Soviet soldiers called some of the survivors into one area and told us we needed to put on our old striped prisoner uniforms.

Bobeshi gasped at the idea of it. Why would we ever want to wear those parasite-infected, soil-soaked uniforms again?

The Soviets explained that they just wanted to film us exiting the camp, to record the moment in history. They had not rolled cameras the day they arrived to liberate us.

It seemed strange. But the soldiers assured us that the striped uniforms had been disinfected and we would only be wearing them for a short time. It was the dead of winter and very cold outside, so we were allowed to wear many layers under our uniforms. These soldiers worried about our safety.

"*Davay ya tebe pomogu,*" an officer said to me in Russian as I exited the barracks dressed in three layers and one very oversized blue-and-gray-striped prisoner shirt. He was offering to help me. He buttoned up my prisoner shirt and took me from my grandmother.

I'm sure she must have tried to stop him. Bobeshi was my sole protector. She wouldn't want me out of her reach. But in the end every prisoner was forced to trust the Soviets. They lined up a group of small children—a few dozen who had survived the largest and most notorious death camp in history. "Pull up your shirtsleeves and show us your numbers," a Soviet soldier directed as his camera rolled. I didn't understand Russian. *"Pokaz mi twoj reka,"* a translator tried again in Polish, making gestures. Like the children around me, I rolled up the sleeve of my oversized striped prisoner shirt and displayed my tattoo.

I didn't realize it then, but that footage would eventually remind millions of people around the world of the atrocities of the Holocaust. One day I, too, would watch those images on a screen and be stunned at seeing myself, dressed in prisoner stripes amid a tiny club of Auschwitz's best hiders.

20

HOME

Not long after this, Bobeshi got word that arrangements had been made.

"Michael, we're going to Żarki!" she said with a wide smile on the day we were leaving Auschwitz forever. "Wait until you see our house. Your big living room—it's the size of three elders' quarters glued together." She explained there was an extra-large front window and that I would have my own bedroom in the house, too.

We were in an office at the camp, awaiting instructions. Bobeshi scrounged up a pencil and drew me a picture of the house on paper. "Here's your bed. And there was a bed for Samuel, of course." She sighed deeply. "Now I suppose I'll sleep there with you. Then we can never be lonely, right?" she said rather convincingly.

Hearing Samuel's name reminded me of that long train

ride we had taken together six months earlier. I was picturing his pained face as he crouched down, jammed between people on the train car from Pionki to Auschwitz. His brown hair was hanging over his eyes. Wait—was his hair brown or blond? Why couldn't I remember?

The more I tried to picture Samuel's hair color, the more I lost the image of him in my mind.

My memory was broken.

I tried to recall my other family members who were missing.

"Bobeshi, Papa had curls just like me, didn't he?"

I started to cry as I tried to capture other memories.

What was that song Mami always sang to me and Samuel? *"Zog nit keinmal . . ."* I couldn't recall the chorus.

I tried to remember how Mamishu smelled when she came home from the ammunitions factory at night.

Did Samuel keep a big pile of rocks hidden under his pillow at Pionki? I think I remembered that!

But what was Papa's nickname for me?

Questions like these dribbled out in an endless string as Bobeshi pulled me beside her on a spindle-back bench in the old SS office. She looked inside the satchel she was carrying, making sure she had packed all the items of clothing and toiletries the Soviet soldiers had given her for the journey. She had already checked and rechecked the bag at least ten times. She had extra food rations tucked in her brassiere in case someone took her bag.

"Michael," she said. She was using her soft, storytelling voice. "We have hours and hours to talk ahead of us, *zeisele*. I am going to tell you all about your family."

She promised that by the time we got to Żarki I would have a perfect picture of my whole family tree in my mind.

A Soviet soldier handed us paperwork, and then another man led us on a long walk to the train stop outside the gates of Auschwitz.

We boarded a train car that was nothing like the one that had brought us to the camp. There were glass windows and wooden benches and even some empty seats. We had several bottles of water to share for the ride.

The train stopped periodically and we picked up more passengers and stretched our legs at each stop.

And just as she had promised, Bobeshi told me all about my family as the train car rolled slowly on its tracks through fields sprinkled with snow dust in southern Poland.

"Your older brother, Samuel, told Mamishu he wanted a baby brother. He did not want a sister." Bobeshi smiled sadly. "And when you were born he treated you like his toy. Samuel would sneak you out of your crib after your mami had laid you down for the night. Sometimes he would turn an empty box upside down in your room and call it your school desk. Samuel would set you up on the box like a doll and pretend he was the teacher and you were his student—and you couldn't even speak a word yet. Your mamishu would scold him whenever she discovered him doing this. 'You can't wake the *beybi*!' she would yell. Then she'd deposit you back in your crib, tuck Samuel under his blankets, and close the door, waiting to laugh with the rest of us until the door was tightly shut."

This story has stayed in my head all these years. Bobeshi told me others like it all the way to Żarki.

We rode the slow-moving train northward for what felt like a long time, snacking on crackers and hard candies that the soldiers had given us. The sun still hadn't set yet when we arrived at the train station not far from Żarki. A refugee agency had arranged for a driver who would take us the rest of the way into town. A Polish peasant greeted us warmly from beside his farm wagon.

"Welcome home," he said to my grandmother. "I understand you've been through, erm, a long journey." He looked relieved to have found the right words. "Shall I take your bag?" the man asked as he reached for Bobeshi's satchel.

She clutched it to her chest and said nothing. It was like

she had forgotten how to speak. Bobeshi just helped herself into the back of the old wooden wagon and reached over the edge to yank me up beside her. The driver climbed onto the seat at the front of the wagon and snapped the reins; a skinny horse led the way.

We were on a muddy road that wound its way through dense forests and fields. The views were so peaceful we hardly noticed that the wagon had one wheel smaller than the others, making the cart wobble like a wounded animal trying to run with a bad leg. The familiar landscape must have triggered millions of memories for Bobeshi, because without me even asking, she launched into storytelling once again.

"Your papa had dark eyes and dark skin like me. When he was little, he had shiny brown ringlets that fell to his shoulder, so beautiful I couldn't bear to cut his hair for years," Bobeshi said.

After a moment she chuckled a little, clearly remembering something amusing. She told me that when Samuel was about three years old—not long before the war started—he insisted on helping Papa collect water from the fountain in town on Sunday mornings. "I won't spill one drop this time. I'm going to be so helpful," he would promise. Bobeshi told me my father always relented, much to my mother's chagrin. Mamishu would have preferred that her pails come back full and her son's pants cuffs come back dry. She and Bobeshi would need fresh water to prepare the day's meals. And yet every Sunday morning, Papa would grin in silence as he followed behind Samuel, a little boy with two buckets that tipped and turned as water sloshed at his ankles with each footstep.

Papa would encourage him with a smile on his face. "Yes, you're doing a very good job. You are a big help. Your mother and grandmother will be so pleased."

Bobeshi told me that sometimes Samuel would stop for a rest along the short trip home and he'd tip a half-empty pail toward his lips to sneak a drink, spilling more on his shirtfront.

My grandmother smiled as she recalled how proud Samuel would look as he marched up the front steps, his pails still tipping but with little water left to spill. She and Mamishu tried to hide their frustration—and amusement—when the two Bornstein men returned home with barely a quart of water remaining.

We were getting close to Żarki now, and the area was rich with shadowy woodland. The carriage was hobbling along the road, which cut straight through the thick brush of leafless, low-hanging tree branches. The road was lined with lots of trash and debris. The area was dirtier than I imagined it would be. Bobeshi had talked about this place like it was a paradise.

I could see the outline of buildings far in the distance as I looked down the shaded road. Two-story buildings that, even from far away, looked tired and worn. I could see what appeared to be a church near the structures, but there was nothing impressive about this view. The thick trees around us cast such darkness on the dirt road that only a weblike design played on the ground where sunlight streamed through thinner branches.

Bobeshi told the carriage driver to stop and got down from the wagon before he could help her.

I had heard so many stories about Żarki along the journey that I couldn't help speaking up. "Bobeshi—this isn't home, right? Can't we stay in the wagon?"

Why was I being difficult?

Bobeshi helped me down and sent the driver on his way. I stood looking around. I continued to fuss until, right there in the roadway, Bobeshi slapped my behind very hard. For all the time I had spent in a ghetto and in concentration camps, no one had ever spanked me. No one I loved had ever even raised a voice at me. It stung me into silence.

We stood on that road long after the *clip-clop* of the

horse's hooves had faded into the distance. Bobeshi finally spoke. I don't know if she was talking to me or not. I just listened.

"You're all gone, aren't you? You are all just voices in the wind now, I suppose."

My grandmother stared at the tired town that lay ahead. There was no movement, no one out walking.

"Are you dust and ashes, or are you the air I breathe? Go on, and pull my feet. I can't make them move alone."

I knew Bobeshi was talking crazy, but I wasn't going to interrupt her thoughts again.

This wasn't what I expected at all. As we approached the town we could see old signs on the roadway, facing toward town with the warning: JUDEN! GEH NICHT! STRAFE IST DER TOD! Jews! Do not pass! Punishment is death!

I could read the signs now. Do you remember who had taught me to read? Samuel did. At Pionki, when we would wait for Mamishu, Papa, and Bobeshi to come home from their work assignments, Samuel was my keeper most days. He would point to words as he read to me in German, the language he was learning to speak fluently. He showed me how to sound out the very small words, and I caught on fast.

I should have felt sad remembering Samuel, but instead I suddenly felt light and happy. Not only could I picture his face, but I could remember his voice! In this place, I could recall so much more than I had realized was stored in my brain. In this place, I also felt more certain than ever that Mamishu would reappear.

We walked on to where the woods finally spread open like a curtain opening on a stage. We were in the town of Żarki. The square stood just before us. The square was surrounded by two- and even three-story brick buildings. There was a hair salon that was closed up with boards over the windows and a bakery that also looked like it hadn't had a customer or a loaf of bread in it for years. There was a leather shop—it was closed, too.

"That's where we used to get our meat for the Sabbath meal." Bobeshi pointed to a building with a narrow glass storefront at the corner of the square. There was a hole from a bullet in the glass.

A few scattered townspeople milled about the space—a cluster of men talking and smoking thickly rolled cigars and two young women carrying yokes on their shoulders with two pails of water on either end. The women approached a fountain in the center of the square and filled their buckets each with water. It was, I gathered, the same fountain Bobeshi had spoken of on our journey to town. Żarki had had electric power since 1925 but twenty years later still didn't have a public water supply or sewers. Water splashed lightly on the two women's clothes—their buckets tilting from side to side as they walked away in slow, measured strides. The people stared at us like we'd arrived from another planet.

We walked a little farther and turned down a little street with homes that all shared a common gray coolness in their appearance. Some were short, and some were taller, but all were made of smooth limestone. Weeds and patches of grass grew everywhere. The homes looked broken to me, in comparison to the neatly built structures at Auschwitz.

We stopped in front of one of the larger homes on the block and Bobeshi said, "Do you remember this, Michael?"

I wondered if I should, but I did not.

"This is my home, *libling*. This is your home. It is where we all lived."

She pointed at the wide rectangular window in front. "You used to stand inside that window with your face pressed against the glass, trying to catch a glimpse of Papa coming down the street at night. Mamishu and I always knew when he was near because you would start slapping your hands against the glass in excitement."

I could have sworn I saw some kind of movement inside the window. Maybe it was just a shadow.

Bobeshi nodded toward the right side of the house. "Your room is over there. Samuel used to beg to stay up

late, and you never looked tired. Almost as soon as Mamishu kissed you both goodnight, though, your room fell as
quiet as a synagogue during private reflection. Sometimes
you would both try to stay up and play. You would fight it,
but sleep usually won."

My grandmother started pulling me right up the path to
the front door, excited to discover that our home was still
standing.

As we climbed the paved steps to the front door, I held
close to Bobeshi. The steps had no handrail along the side
and I was afraid I'd fall off the landing.

The wood frame door looked warped and rotted, and
Bobeshi wrinkled her nose at the sight of it. She sighed in a
manner that said, *Ah, not what I had imagined.* Then she
reached for the front doorknob, but it was missing.

This house clearly had stories to tell.

As Bobeshi started pushing the door open, we were suddenly face-to-face with a very large woman, thick and
round. She had bright red hair and fat pink cheeks, and I
would guess she was about the same age as Mamishu.

"What are you doing? You're just going to walk right
into my house and you don't even knock?" Her voice was
shrill and angry.

The redheaded lady was spitting her words, and she

didn't even wipe her mouth as a few droplets of saliva landed on her dimpled chin.

Bobeshi stood straight and tall and said, "Pardon me, but this is *my* home. I lived here for many years before the war. Before—"

My grandmother had to stop and collect herself.

"My son, Israel Bornstein, is—was—the president of the Judenrat, and this is Israel's little boy—"

The woman cut Bobeshi off abruptly, shouting, "You are a Jew? How did you escape the ovens, you slippery woman? You should have cooked with your friends! Now get off my steps before I call the police."

With that, Bobeshi's own front door was slammed in her face.

21

AUNT HILDA

Two women stood in front of the small rural train station in late spring of 1945.

A tall Polish man with pale features leaned down from his carriage to speak with them. "Is one of you Hilda?" he asked.

My aunt—Mamishu's sister—nodded.

"I've been instructed to escort you wherever you need to go. Does your companion need a ride, too?"

Hilda Jonisch was traveling with Abigail, a friend who had looked increasingly ill at ease since the train arrived.

Hilda eyed the man with suspicion. She had not been born a cautious person, but five years of war, one ghetto, and four death camps had made her so.

"I'm being paid to help with transport, ma'am. By the agency. I'll get you both where you're going, without delay."

The agency was the United Nations Relief and Rehabilitation Administration (UNRRA), one of many aid groups that helped concentration camp prisoners get home.

Hilda and her companion had already traveled nearly five hundred kilometers and taken multiple trains to get to this point. The journey from Oschatz, Germany, to the train stop several kilometers from Żarki left her with little energy, and UNRRA officials had told her a carriage would be waiting to help her complete her journey.

There was something soothing and kind in the man's voice and Hilda's shoulders automatically relaxed.

"My name is Nicodem. Friends call me Nico. You can certainly call me Nico." He winked at Hilda, catching her off guard.

Her shoulders tensed back up immediately. Hilda had always drawn attention from men, and her instinct was to worry about his intentions.

Then she remembered how she looked at this moment. She had caught sight of a haggard reflection in the window of the first train that took them here. She was so bony and malnourished that it wasn't until she reached up to pull a strand of hair out of her eyes that she realized the reflection belonged to her. Her hair had thinned from hunger and her cheeks had paled from illness. Surely this man was only aiming to make her feel at ease.

"Fine, then," she said. "My friend Abigail made a late decision to join me. We'll be traveling to Żarki. Do you know the road that takes us there?"

Hilda thought she saw Nico flinch and then quickly recover his composure. "Of course, of course. Climb aboard, ladies."

Nico reached out his hand to help the two young women climb up, but instead they ignored his hand and helped each other onto the empty bench behind him.

As the horses started pulling the carriage down a rocky trail, Abigail suddenly shouted, "Stop! Please, stop!" She looked panicked.

Abigail was barely twenty years old, a decade younger than my aunt. She had no home and no surviving relatives. She and Hilda were family now, though, bonded by unfathomable secrets and horrors.

Hilda had first befriended Abigail in the Majdanek concentration camp near Lublin, roughly five hundred kilometers east of Żarki, and the pair had managed to stay together all the way to the Buchenwald concentration camp. At one camp in between they were assigned to a task they never wished to talk about again in this life. The women were *Sonderkommandos*. Their job, under threat of death, was to remove the corpses of women and children from the gas chambers, women and children they had just seen lining up at roll call only hours earlier. My aunt Hilda was a body pusher.

At Majdanek, they had been assigned to pack ammunition. It was the same job my mother performed at Pionki and the perfect job for women with small, quick fingers.

"I've got a wicked idea," Hilda dared to whisper to Abigail on the first day they met. She explained her idea of "forgetting" to pack every third bullet with gunpowder.

Abigail's face turned white. She was afraid she would be caught whispering on the job. She was even more afraid at the mere suggestion of fouling up under the German guards' close watch.

"You're crazy!" Abigail had whispered back. "What if we're caught?"

Hilda let one tiny giggle escape in a place that knew no humor. "What if we're caught?" Hilda nodded toward the guards at the door. "We're at the Majdanek concentration camp, my friend. I have news for you. We're *already* caught."

Abigail felt herself come alive at the thought of breaking the rules, risking her life in an effort to save perhaps every third life of those who were fighting against the Nazis. More than that, the idea of outsmarting her captors was invigorating.

So it went for many months. Hilda and Abigail reported

for work each morning like obedient lambs. Every third bullet they packed was a dud.

Now here they sat, two years later, bonded through all they had endured together.

"What's the matter, miss?" Nico asked Abigail as he brought the carriage to an abrupt stop.

"Hilda, I love you—you are my kindred spirit," Abigail said. "But I can't go with you. You're returning home; you have people waiting for you." Abigail explained that she realized in this moment that she needed to find her own way. She had a cousin named Adam who had left for America before the war; maybe she could find a way to get a travel visa to join him. She said her mind had been swaying every which way during this journey, and now staying with Hilda didn't feel right. "My fate lies elsewhere. I had to come this far to know it. I'm going back to the agency."

Tears were streaming down Abigail's face now, but her voice was resolute. Even as Hilda tried to protest, Abigail stayed firm.

"If you and your family ever come to America, you can look for me. I'll be married to a wealthy businessman, eating decadent meals by a fireplace at night," she said with a laugh. "My children will be singing happy songs. Not the ghetto songs we know and love, right?"

After a sad farewell between the two friends, Abigail stepped down from the carriage and began walking back to the station. Aunt Hilda was sure she even saw Nico swallow back tears before he snapped the reins. The carriage set off again, bound for Żarki.

A long silence passed before Nico finally spoke. "So your name is Hilda. I got that part. What's the rest of your story? You look like you have one."

Hilda was horrified just thinking about how she could find the words if she actually did tell anyone her story. No language could be sufficient to describe all the terrible things she had seen. "Never mind me," she shot back. "What's *your* story?"

"All right, I'll talk," Nico said with a gentle smile.

There was a lightness about him that Hilda vaguely remembered existing in herself, once upon a time.

Nico said he was from Krakow. He used to own a small metal workshop before the war. He made tools and hardware, that sort of thing. The shop was his dream. He had saved for years and convinced his parents to invest in the business, too. In one fiery moment, the whole space was destroyed. A bomb from the Luftwaffe, the German air force.

"I'm not going to sit here and snivel about it to you, though. I can see my troubles are nil, by comparison."

Nico paused, waiting to see if Hilda might say something in response, but she didn't. So the man just talked
and talked, passing the time for both of them.

It was a welcome distraction for Hilda, who continued
to find the sound of his voice comforting. This stranger
gave her a measure of protection she rarely felt.

It had been years since her husband, Joseph Wygocka,
had left Poland for America. Many months before the first
bombs fell, when war seemed on the horizon, he'd packed a
large suitcase and announced he was leaving. He had said
he would send for Hilda and her family, but he hadn't.
Hilda was in her early twenties when Joseph left, and she
assumed she would spend the rest of her life alone.

From the way Nico looked over a broad shoulder to nod
her way or smile at her as he told his stories, some strange,
foreign feeling came to her. It was hope. Maybe life could
start anew now. Maybe.

A palpable connection formed between the driver and
Hilda. Maybe that's why, before the end of the trip, Nico
decided he had to warn her. They were just minutes away
from reaching Żarki.

"Hilda, I have to tell you something." He drew a deep
breath, like he was trying to inhale courage. "Your town . . .
such a nice town. I used to have business dealings there and

visited many times. Well, your town took a big hit in the war. I hope you understand—"

"Oh, I know," Hilda interrupted. She knew how bad Żarki looked. She had been there once before to see the damage left by the German bombing. It was the people she longed to see, not the architecture. The Gestapo had allowed many members of her family to stay behind in the ghetto, she explained. "My brother-in-law was an important person. He had influence."

From the Żarki ghetto, the open ghetto, Mamishu had been able to get several letters smuggled north into Warsaw, so she had communicated with her sister. Hilda knew all about Papa's Judenrat position.

"Hilda, listen to me. The Germans—they cleared out the ghetto in the fall of '42." Nico said the whole community had been eradicated. Not one Jewish soul was left behind.

He looked over his shoulder just as Hilda slumped forward, bowed down by his news. Then he pulled the reins and brought the carriage to a deliberate stop.

"No, please. Say that's not true," Hilda said.

Nico could not comfort her. He could only tell her that he'd heard a crazy story through some friends in Częstochowa: a whole community was eliminated, yet several members of one family had returned. "Their last name started with a *J*, I think." Nico paused and then said, "Yes, the Jonisch family."

When she recovered from the shock of hearing this, my aunt reintroduced herself to her carriage driver. "Nico, my name is Hilda," she said. "Hilda Jonisch."

She asked the stunned driver to please continue their journey to Żarki as quickly as possible.

22

GHOSTFACE

"**Bobeshi, why do we always** cross the street when we go past the gray house on the corner?"

Bobeshi shook her head at me as we walked home from the Żarki market. "Oh, Michael, let's just say bad things happened to the family who once lived in that house. I like to put a little distance there."

Although I didn't know it at the time, it was the house of the Beritzmann family, the ones my mother had seen being executed in the graveyard on Bloody Monday, more than five years earlier.

"Speaking of distance, Michael, we have quite a ways to go and you need to pick up those feet."

We did have a long walk ahead of us, down a narrow, dusty road and through a thick patch of woodland. Bobeshi carefully watched her feet as we walked so that she wouldn't trip over stones and sticks. We walked all the way to a gravel road that led to the abandoned farm we had called home from the end of winter.

After we had discovered that the Bornstein family house in town was occupied and that Jews' homecomings weren't being celebrated by some Polish townspeople in Żarki, Bobeshi had decided we were safest on the outskirts of town.

There was a covered chicken coop on the farm that was in better shape than the farmhouse. Pear trees already bloomed on the property, unaware that it was too early in the season for such growth. It was as if they were flowering just for us. Now that spring had come, it wasn't so cold outside, either, and our nights of slumber on straw thickly laid over a dirt floor were fairly comfortable.

To look for work, Bobeshi would tiptoe out of the structure early some mornings, hoping I wouldn't be disturbed—but I always woke. In town she was hired for odd jobs, sweeping sidewalks outside businesses or cleaning storefront windows. Just like at Auschwitz, she would tell me, "Wait right here and don't make a sound. I promise I will return to you."

She always did.

"Can I play at Ruth's house tomorrow?" I asked as our

farm came into sight. "I'll wake up extra early, Bobeshi. I won't make a fuss about the long walk either."

We were some of the luckiest people in Żarki. Not only had we survived the Auschwitz death camp, but we had returned to find cousins and uncles waiting to embrace us. They were stunned to open the front door of the Jonisch family home and see us standing there, ragged and worn. Bobeshi was equally stunned to see them.

I hadn't remembered my cousin Ruth, the one who had been kept safe in the orphanage. I didn't remember Uncle David or Uncle Sam or Uncle Moniek either. Aunt Cecia was a stranger. But my uncle Mullek—his face looked so much like my own and my mother's, blue eyes and all.

"I could be mistaken for your father, couldn't I, little Michael?" he had said to me when Bobeshi and I appeared at the front door. Then Mullek cringed, realizing the implications of what he'd said.

I had, however, grown accustomed to knowing that Papa and Samuel were gone. Still, I wanted Mamishu. And I wanted company during the day. I hated being alone in the chicken coop while Bobeshi swept streets in the square. Sometimes my grandmother would wake me early and take me to play with Ruth.

Truthfully, I was a little annoyed at Bobeshi for not just moving in with my mother's family.

"Oh, no, Cecia," Bobeshi had told my aunt. "We're quite comfortable at the farm, and we enjoy our privacy, don't we, Michael?" Her expression warned me not to respond, as nobody knew we weren't actually living in a proper house.

The Jonisches weren't Bobeshi's blood relatives. Plus, my uncles, another aunt, and two distant cousins had squeezed into the home already. Bobeshi preferred to keep to herself, even if it meant abandoning me in an empty chicken coop most days.

Sometimes when I was alone, I would daydream that Mamishu would be walking side by side with Bobeshi as they turned up the gravel road to the farmhouse at the end of the day. *Mamishu, you came back!* I would shout. Then I would run down the road into my mother's arms. She would pick me up, not realizing I had grown too big to be carried anymore, and kiss my cheeks and my head.

On this day, though, there was no time for daydreaming. Bobeshi had finished work early and returned for me. We had traveled to the market to buy supplies for a special Shabbat meal with Mamishu's family. We had to arrive by sundown to light the candles and welcome in the Sabbath.

I loved to be with my family. I had no concept of how

strange it was that so many of my relatives were still alive. The Germans had tried to "clean" the town of Jews, but that night almost every chair would be filled in the Jonisch home.

We hurried into the chicken coop, and Bobeshi handed me the clean wool pants and white cotton shirt she had saved for two weeks to buy me. The pants fit me perfectly, unlike the stiff trousers the Allied soldiers had given me as I departed Auschwitz. Bobeshi said I looked handsome.

Dressed and ready, I practically skipped back down the gravel road and through the thicket path toward the Jonisch house that night, imagining a delicious Shabbat dinner.

The sun was close to setting. As we approached the house we could make out the figures of about six people gathered on the front porch, talking excitedly.

I knew one of those voices well. It was a woman's voice— and it didn't belong to Aunt Cecia, whose register was soft and low. No—this was a higher voice that made my knees feel weak.

"Mullek, you've never been so thin in all your life. Where's that round belly of yours? Wartime suits you!" said the familiar voice.

The family was chuckling. I could see as Bobeshi and I got closer that my uncle David's arm was around the woman's shoulders. I could only see her profile, though. Her stance, her movements, her voice—*Mamishu*. She had returned, and I was the only person who had never given up. I knew she would be back.

"Mamishu!" I screamed wildly. "Mamishu, Mamishu!"

I was crying and shouting at the same time.

Bobeshi tried to squeeze my hand tighter, but I ripped it away from her and started running.

The whole family turned to see me flying down Sosnowa Street. The woman turned. Only—her face wasn't right. I mean, it looked like my mother's, with a soft, rounded chin and deep-set eyes. Her hair and her eyebrows were dark, though, like a frame that was never there before. She was like a ghost of my mother.

"Michael, my Michael!" the ghost screamed in my direction. "Come to me, my sweet boy. How I've longed to meet you! How I've thought of you, my darling. But I'm not your mami. No, baby, I'm not."

The woman was dashing toward the spot where I had stopped cold in my tracks. Her arms were open wide like she was going to lift me up and hug me, just like Mamishu was meant to do. She even carried the same scent as my mother. It was terrifyingly eerie how a stranger could seem so familiar.

I put my hand up in the universal sign for *stop*. "Who *are* you?" I asked in as strong a voice as I could muster.

"My *libling*, I know you don't know me. I'm your aunt Hilda. Your mami is my big sister and my best friend." She touched my arm just as Bobeshi caught up to us in the middle of the road. "Hello, Dora," she said, greeting my grandmother with a big smile before turning her attention back to me. "I've dreamed of seeing you for a very long time, Michael. Your mother told me all about you in letters she wrote."

I can't describe the instant feeling of betrayal that left my insides numb. I felt robbed of a moment. I felt tricked. I had no clue who Aunt Hilda was. I guess Bobeshi had mentioned her once or twice in stories, but this woman was a stranger to me.

Still, when this woman, ignoring my tantrum, pulled me in close for a hug, I felt safer than I had in a very long time. Bobeshi had protected my life at all costs. Protecting my heart, though, hadn't been her natural instinct.

I buried my face in Aunt Hilda's chest and cried hard. When I finally calmed down, she took my hand and led me back to Aunt Cecia's house. Bobeshi had gone ahead and was waiting on the porch with the others. She had given Aunt Hilda the space to calm me down because she knew we both needed it.

"I see you and your aunt have been getting acquainted, Michael," Cecia said. "Now you and Ruth must go wash your hands. It's time to sit down for the holiday meal. Prayers will begin in a moment, *zeisele*."

I splashed water on my face from a container in the kitchen, embarrassed that I had cried so hard and eager to wash away the evidence.

When I stepped into the living room moments later, there was already chanting and prayer. Candles were lit and everyone was deep in reflection. This was not any ordinary Shabbat meal. This was a special time in more ways than one.

On May 7, 1945, a German general representing the country's high command had signed an unconditional surrender agreement with the United States, Britain, Russia, and the other Allies. The war in Europe was formally over. The Nazis were defeated.

As the men in my family stood and rocked their weight from their heels to their toes in prayer, my stomach growled. I had gotten good at muting out hunger when I was in Auschwitz, but somehow back in Żarki hunger pained me.

"Can we eat a little something now?" I whispered to Aunt Hilda, who insisted I sit on her lap like a baby. I hadn't known her long—but I was aware that if I was going to ask anyone questions during prayer, she would be the only person who wouldn't yell at me for my impatience.

"I need to fetch some water from the kitchen," Hilda said loudly. She jumped up from her seat, bumping me onto my feet. "Come, Michael, you'll help your auntie," she said with a wink. Then she whispered across the table to Ruth, who was just my age, "Ruth, I mean, Kristina, darling. Come and help me, too, *libling*," she coaxed.

But I knew Ruth wouldn't come. She never left her mother's side.

"Okay, then," Aunt Hilda said. "We'll be right back."

Off we went to the kitchen, where, behind the closed door, Aunt Hilda slipped me a piece of flat bread meant for the meal.

I nibbled on the crumbling corners. I felt a little heart-sick suddenly but also couldn't resist a small bite. I didn't want to wait for prayers to be finished so we could eat.

"Don't tell on me, Michael. It'll be our secret!" Aunt Hilda said.

She kissed me on top of my head the same way Mamishu always had. I tried not to cry, but my eyes didn't listen to my head. They started welling up with tears.

"What is it, Michael? You know, I have seen what you have seen. You can tell me anything."

"Aunt Hilda, do you think my mother could still be alive? Why is Bobeshi so certain she is gone? Mamishu told me we would see each other one day when we were free."

Hilda exhaled deeply.

I looked right into her eyes, hoping she would be forced to speak honestly. "Please, Aunt Hilda. What did everyone tell you? Where did Mamishu go?"

"Sophie—your mother—was sent to a labor camp in Austria. I don't know anything about her work assignments. I only know that your grandmother learned there was a fire. Michael, the labor camp where your mami was taken—it burned down. No prisoners were said to have survived." Now Hilda's eyes pooled with tears. "I don't know, though, *libling*. I guess no one can say for sure that she was inside those gates when the fire burned. If you want me to tell you that your mami could come back one day—well, I can't say that she won't."

My heart swelled for a second.

Aunt Hilda kept talking. "No one could have guessed I would have returned to Żarki. Yet here I am and here we all are . . . thirteen around the table for a special Shabbat!" She patted my head and seemed to daydream of Mamishu for a moment, too. "Anything is possible, I suppose, Michael. For now, though, let's celebrate what we have."

Aunt Hilda let me take one last nibble of the flat bread while she refilled a pitcher of water. Finally, we returned to the dinner table, which was temporarily in the living room. There were simply too many guests to squeeze into the dining room, after all.

23

A KNOCK AT THE DOOR

"I can't wait. Please, Bobeshi. Can we go right now?"

It was lunchtime, but I was too impatient to eat.

Two weeks after the family had last gathered, Bobeshi agreed to let me have a sleepover at Cousin Ruth's house. The mosquitoes were biting terribly at the farm. I was looking forward to sleeping in the shelter of a house with proper windows and doors to keep away the bugs. Plus, Aunt Hilda was sleeping on the floor in Ruth's bedroom now, and she had promised to tell us three bedtime stories, even after Aunt Cecia had tucked us in.

It was Shabbat again, so we would be eating dinner in the glow of the Sabbath candles and there would be kosher wine to taste. Truthfully, I thought wine tasted disgusting. It was clear it was a privilege for us to drink it, though, so Ruth and I always pressed the cup to our lips and let a droplet of alcohol sear our mouths as it was passed around. We licked our lips like it was a treat.

"*L'chaim!*" we would all toast. To life! Jews have always said *L'chaim* around the Shabbat table, but these days a toast to life carried extra meaning.

Under the strain of my constant begging, Bobeshi finally relented and took me to Aunt Cecia's early that Friday. However, she insisted that she couldn't stay for the dinner herself.

"Oh, thank you, Cecia. It's so kind of you to always invite me, but you know I'm tired these days. I'll honor the Sabbath back at my house"—meaning our chicken coop—"and I won't be lonely at all"—meaning she'd be lonely every second. "I thank you for taking Michael. He's very excited to be with you all, and I will enjoy some extra sleep in the morning."

Bobeshi left me—and a basket of spring flowers—on my relatives' porch and said goodbye.

I won't lie to you. I was glad to have a break from Bobeshi. To me, she seemed sad all the time after Auschwitz. It's hard to be with someone who is always sad. I loved my grandmother, but I was not quite five years old and I needed a cheerful respite.

Shabbat with my relatives felt glorious. Aunt Cecia lit

the candles and covered her eyes, waving her hands inward three times to invite the Sabbath queen into her home—a spiritual queen, of course.

But as if on cue, there was a loud knock at the door at just that moment.

Uncle David blew out the fresh-lit candles. In neighboring towns, bands of anti-Semitic ruffians had gone door-to-door looking for Jews who had returned from camps to heckle them, hound them, and sometimes beat them for sport. If they had reached Żarki, seeing signs of a Jewish ceremony in progress might only incite them further.

"Cecia, hide the challah plate in the flour bag! David, the candles! Don't just blow them out—*hide* them." My uncle Sam shouted orders as quietly as a man can shout. "Michael and Ruth—I mean, Kristina—hurry to the bedroom and tuck yourselves under the covers. Don't make a sound. Now!"

I froze for just a second, panicked by the tone in my uncle's voice. I looked at Aunt Hilda for reassurance, but her face provided none.

Finally, Ruth grabbed me by the sleeve of my new white button-front shirt and pulled me up the stairs to her room. I instinctively dived under the bed. There was a long dust ruffle that pooled on the floor around the bedframe, creating a perfect hiding place. When you spend time in Auschwitz, you're quick to look for the sneakiest, safest spot.

Ruth did as she was told, of course. She always did. She tucked herself under the covers of her bed, whimpering. She wasn't pretending. Ruth often cried when she had to leave her mother's side—even inside the same house.

Downstairs, our family swept the room for evidence of Jewish tradition in a frantic thirty-second rush to hide religious relics.

Then Uncle Sam opened the front door.

The details of what happened next became a story Aunt Cecia would recount again and again in the years to come.

Standing just outside the threshold were five men who could best be described as mean-looking. Their eyes were small and squinted, their jaws were clenched like they were ready for a fight, and their hands were balled into fists before Uncle Sam even said good evening.

"Smells like a holiday in here," one man said. "We don't appreciate you filthy Jew-rats celebrating in a place where you no longer belong."

Another one of the angry men pushed his way into the house and glared into Uncle Moniek's eyes. "You and your synagogues and your black-magic candles—you invited the enemy in. The only good the Germans did in this war was to drive your people out of Poland."

A third man had entered and grabbed Uncle David by the shirt collar, and it was clear these men came to fight, maybe to kill.

But then the men met their match. Aunt Hilda had not survived the Warsaw ghetto and numerous death camps to be brutalized by five bitter countrymen with a misplaced grudge.

"Gentlemen, I think you are confused," Hilda said, pushing her way out of the kitchen where my uncles had urged her and Cecia to wait. She almost gasped when she saw the size of these men, each one towering over my uncles. The apparent leader of the group had an oddly shaped dark brown mole on one cheek, and his eyes looked venomous. She had committed to this instinctive plan, though, and it was too late to turn back.

"This is hardly a Jewish home." Hilda spit at the floor as if she were disgusted by the thought. "Quite the contrary, we are as Catholic as any of you. Why, my niece just said her evening prayers by Saint Antiochus and tucked her rosary beads away. Here, have a look."

Aunt Hilda drew the men into the living room. Their faces still appeared angry, but their hands were now unclenched. Hilda pulled a long wooden set of rosary beads from the side table next to the sofa and kissed them softly.

"Come," she said, beckoning the men up the stairs toward the bedrooms. "Our darling Kristina can't have fallen asleep with all this noise. She would love to recite her prayers for you."

Uncle Sam was surely panicked at the invitation to draw these men farther into his home, but there was no way to protest now.

The faces of the men changed visibly as they turned the corner, one by one—packing into the entrance of Ruth's bedroom. There, over Ruth's bed, hung a large wooden cross with the image of Jesus carved into the front—while I lay silent and motionless under the dust ruffle.

Uncle Sam and Aunt Cecia had placed the crucifix there as soon as they returned to their home with Ruth, who had spent her formative years being raised by nuns. They didn't want her transition to be marred by angst or guilt and had worried that Ruth might feel lost without the religion that had guided her at the orphanage. They loved their own religion—they cherished Judaism with all their hearts—but they loved Ruth more. So in the interest of making her happy and comfortable, they let her keep the rosary beads the nuns had given her and even encouraged her to say her evening prayers to Jesus.

"What are you doing hanging that symbol of Catholicism over her bed?" Uncle David had said with disgust in his voice the day the wooden cross went up on the wall.

"This is *my* house—and Ruth is *my* daughter," Cecia had hurled back. "You may live here or not live here. But that cross is staying up for as long as my daughter needs it there."

Who could have guessed the cross would be a lifesaver only a short while later?

"Gentlemen, I do understand why you might have been misled. This is, after all, the section of town that was once filled with only Jews. This home was empty, so we figured it should not go to waste. Our own homes near the church were destroyed by bombings. So here we are, living where all the Jews used to live." Hilda wrinkled her nose in another show of mock disgust. "Perhaps you would like to hear Kristina recite her evening prayer again. You look like you could use a blessing yourselves." She pushed her way through the men, who were now open-mouthed and embarrassed. I could see them through the lace holes of the dust ruffle, but they couldn't see me.

Hilda carefully folded back the sheets until just Ruth's little face was showing. She still had tears in her eyes. "What's the matter, Kristina? Did you get scared with all the strange voices? Hush, my darling. We just hoped you would say a nice prayer for these men."

Hilda leaned down to kiss Ruth's wet cheek and then helped her out of bed. Ruth knelt on the floor at the foot of the bed. I was scared that her knees might kick the bedskirt in and I would be discovered.

I didn't know any Catholic prayers—that's for sure. My language now was a messy mix of Yiddish, Polish, and even some German I had picked up by listening to guards and soldiers.

Fortunately, Ruth was as smart and meticulous as ever. She had been careful not to ruffle the bedskirt as she took her place.

"O only begotten word of the Father, Jesus Christ, who alone are perfect: according to the greatness of your mercy, do not abandon me, your servant, but ever rest in my heart . . ."

The prayer went on and on, but Ruth's Polish was flawless and her recitation would have made any nun proud. At this moment, it certainly made her family proud, because as Ruth recited, one of the angry men began to weep.

After the prayer ended, their leader apologized. He explained that the one bit of good Nazi soldiers did in their country had been undone in some places: Jews had been coming back. "We just want to guarantee that anyone who thinks they're going to invade our towns again with their black hats and long coats knows they aren't welcome."

Another of the strangers jumped in, saying, "But instead it looks like we invaded your good Catholic home. May Christ forgive us."

The other men followed suit with sincere apologies.

They promised not to bother my family again. The last to leave through the bedroom door—the man with the mole—turned back around to say, "Goodnight, Kristina. Sleep well, child."

Ruth slipped back under the covers and waited until the strangers' voices faded away from outside the house.

Then she bent her body off the side of the bed and pulled up the lacy white dust ruffle, exhaling a soft giggle. "You can come out now, scaredy cat," she said with a smirk.

We scurried through the hall and down the steps to our elder relatives, who were waiting for us to appear. They looked emotionally worn.

Hilda summoned some sincere enthusiasm. "You, my *libling*, were simply marvelous! Kristina-Ruth, your prayers went straight to God's ears tonight, darling. Do you know that you saved us all?"

Uncle Moniek turned to me. "Oh, and we can't forget you, little Michael! Where were you hiding all that time?

Even Hilda couldn't tell. Were you in the closet or under the bed? We didn't hear a sound!"

I told them I was right under Ruth's bed, holding my breath. I didn't tell them I had almost laughed when Ruth started chanting those prayers in her perfect Polish.

Within minutes we were again sitting around the Sabbath table. We didn't dare relight the candles, but we said the blessing over the wine and the homemade challah and passed both around for all to sample.

Uncle Sam stopped his brother Moniek just as he was reaching to take a first helping of food on the table.

"It's been quite a night," Sam said from the head of the table. "Shall we all take a moment to reflect and say a silent prayer of gratitude?" I don't know what Sam wanted us to say in our prayers exactly, but I bowed my head and shut my eyes tight and I said this simple prayer over and over again in my head: *Mamishu, please come back. Mamishu, please come back. Mamishu, please come back.*

When I confided my prayer to Hilda at bedtime, she simply said, "Darling, I was wishing for the very same thing. Do you know? Every single person at the Shabbat table tonight shares that wish."

24

A SPLASH OF YELLOW IN ŻARKI

"The men didn't even hear me! Their feet were *this* close to my nose, Bobeshi." I held my two pointer fingers just inches apart as I boasted to my grandmother.

I had been so excited to tell her about the intruders at Uncle Sam's house that I forgot to wish her *Shabbat shalom* (peaceful Sabbath) when my uncle delivered me back to the farm the next day.

Saturday afternoon at the chicken coop seemed dreary after a night in a real bed inside a real bedroom in a real house. It didn't help that it was raining outside and a leak in the roof had created a muddy crater in one corner.

"That sounds like quite an evening. I'm not sorry I missed it." Bobeshi gave as much a smile as she could muster these days. "Goodness knows I am too old to hide under beds, and too forthright to tell a good lie. Now,

Michael—it is still the Sabbath. The sun has not yet set below the horizon. Come, sit with me and let's say the Havdalah prayers." These were part of the ceremony in which we bid the Sabbath farewell.

All business—Bobeshi was really all business. I sighed, following her to the place at the back of the coop where a special twisted candle was ready to be lit.

"*Baruch atah Adonai, Eloheinu melech haolam, borei m'orei ha-eish.*"

We recited the prayer over the light and continued on with prayers for the ceremonial spices and the wine. For this part of the ceremony, Bobeshi filled an old ceramic cup she had found discarded in the woods near the property. We didn't have any family keepsakes anymore with which to honor the Sabbath.

After a simple meal, I fell asleep quickly on my make-shift bed of straw, wool blankets, and a pillow from Aunt Cecia's house. I was still tired from the sleepover there.

A few days later, I awoke with a rumble in my stomach. I hounded Bobeshi until she finally crawled out from under her blankets, too.

"Let's go to town! Do you remember, Bobeshi?"

I had gotten my first taste of tiny wild strawberries when we were last at the market square. My grandmother had stopped at a fruit stand run by a man named Oskar and used all the zlotys she had to buy me a paper bag full of the delectable fruit.

Bobeshi worried about me and loved to see me eat. I still weighed what a toddler should weigh. Though I had grown in height, there was little meat on my bones and my hair just wouldn't grow back. So when Bobeshi saw me polish off that bag of strawberries—and then stick my whole face in the empty bag just to inhale the scent of them—she had promised we would return for more.

"All right, my early bird," Bobeshi sighed. "I'll get up. Just let your old grandmother lie here five more minutes and I'll take you for your berries, Michael."

I agreed. And just to earn some good favor I even busied myself cleaning out the malodorous chamber pot in the far corner of the coop, carrying the metal pail outside carefully and turning its rank contents upside down in the wild poppy fields.

But within seconds of returning, I was hounding my poor grandmother again until she put on her gray sweater—one she had taken from the Kanada warehouse at Auschwitz. She pulled long brown stockings over her legs, covering the bright veins that ran up her calves like lightning bolts. "One bag of strawberries, coming up for my hungry boy," Bobeshi said wearily. "Let's be off."

It was about a thirty-minute walk to town—at Bobeshi's

pace, anyway. We walked down a gravel path, through the wooded trail of stones and boulders, and along the dusty road that took us back to my family's old neighborhood. As we strolled slowly, I busied myself by yanking up yellow dandelions that grew in the tall grass alongside the road. I tangled and twisted the stems into knots, tying the weeds together to make a long chain.

Suddenly, the warmest and cheeriest feeling streaked through my body like someone had just painted me with happiness from my head to my toes. That always happened when a really tangible memory of my mother crossed my mind. I recalled her with a homemade dandelion bracelet around her wrist. Maybe my brother, Samuel, had made it for her—except my mother loved bright colors so much she might have made the little flower chain herself.

"A little splash of yellow makes every day happier." I'm pretty sure she said that more than once.

"Dress happy, and you'll feel happy," Mamishu told our neighbor at Pionki one day when she was using the reflection from the window to apply a coat of bootleg rouge on her cheeks.

I kept on tying dandelions all the way to the market. "Look, Bobeshi! Look how long!" I said proudly, holding out the yellow chain of weeds between my outstretched hands.

"Uh-huh" was all the enthusiasm my grandmother could summon.

It was an overcast day, and all of Żarki looked a little depressed. I don't know why I was such a ball of energy.

When we were not far away from the city center, though, it was clear the market was as energized as I was today. It was a busy day near the Church of Saint Simon, and it looked like everybody in town had stopped to make a purchase. The town was still desolate, of course, compared to what it used to be. Żarki had been two-thirds Jewish, so now much of the population was dead and gone.

But today Żarki was showing signs of life. There was a queue at Oskar's fruit stand. I looked up at Bobeshi with frustration. My grandmother wasn't looking at the strawberry seller, though. Her eyes were carefully tracking a rickety carriage that was pulling up nearby, led by a single white-speckled horse.

I stared, too. I stared hard. I blinked my eyes to clear their focus. What I thought I was seeing had to be imagined. I swallowed hard to prepare for disappointment. The profile of the woman on board, sitting just next to the driver, looked exactly like Mamishu's. I felt none of the confusion I'd had on meeting Aunt Hilda. This woman's features matched my mother's with precision.

It's a tired expression to say that sometimes a person

can feel when eyes are upon her, but that's what seemed to happen. After a few seconds of my staring straight at her, the woman turned and looked right back at me in the crowd.

At that moment, she slapped the driver's arm, causing him to flinch and momentarily speed up the carriage. "Stop!" I could faintly hear her scream over the din of the crowd. "Stop! Stop!"

The woman sprang off the seat like it was a trampoline, landing on the roadway below. The carriage was still coming to a stop beside her. She ran at me, pushing through clusters of people to get to my clenched body. I was paralyzed in space, clutching Bobeshi's hand.

Mamishu?

Maybe it took fifteen seconds for her to get to me. It felt longer.

"Michael, it's me! It's me! It's me!" she cried as she pushed back the people in her way like they were tree branches in a dense forest. "I'm here! It's me!" she just kept shouting as I stood frozen in disbelief.

Her hair was scraggly and fine, and her skin was even more sallow than it had appeared in Auschwitz—but I could have sworn at that moment I would never again see a more beautiful or more comforting sight.

What I felt when Mamishu enveloped me in her arms was too much joy for words. I don't know how to explain it. If we had both seen more sorrow than the world knew it could hold—then this moment was the opposite of that. This was the *opposite* of despair.

Mamishu was on her knees, kissing my cheeks and the top of my bald head.

And Bobeshi was wrapped around the both of us now. She was crying. I was crying, too, but I had never heard of anyone crying from happiness before, so the earthquake of emotion was all the more overwhelming. When I opened my eyes and lifted my head from my mother's shoulder, I saw people standing all around us, staring.

One woman stepped forward and touched my mother's arm. I didn't recognize her—she was a maid who had apparently worked in my parents' home before I was born.

"Welcome home, Mrs. Bornstein," she said softly. She wasn't the only person in the crowd who seemed moved by our reunion. A handful of others were wiping away tears— touched by the miracle of this moment. Mamishu, Bobeshi, and I—we who should all have been dead.

"Michael, you are alive? You are alive!" Mamishu was incredulous. "I should have known," she said as she pulled away from me briefly and inspected me from head to toe.

She straightened my new shirt so that the seams at the top of the arms sat perfectly on my shoulders. I delighted in that motherly gesture. There is no touch on earth as tender as the touch of your own mother.

Mamishu kissed my bald head again and again. Then she pulled back for a better look at my face. "You knew I was coming back for you, yes?" Mamishu asked. Her blue eyes were wet with tears.

"I knew," I said. I dropped my cheek back onto her shoulder softly. I *had* known. I had always believed my mother was alive, and as stunned as I was to be reunited with her on that day, it also felt exactly right. It fit with the picture that had been in my head.

25

SURVIVORS CLUB

I couldn't wait to bring my mother to see the family. Her brothers would be shocked. Maybe I might see them cry with joy. Aunt Cecia, Mamishu's sister-in-law, would be clapping her hands and dancing in excitement.

Aunt Hilda, though, would be the happiest of all. In the short time since she had returned, Aunt Hilda talked to me every day that I saw her about my mother. We both had maintained hope that Mamishu could return home someday. But I knew Aunt Hilda would be speechless to see her lovely Sophie walk through the door.

"How did you survive?" Bobeshi's voice crackled with emotion. She was standing next to us now, wiping her eyes. "I thought—well, Alida and the other women—we heard you had been taken to a work camp in Austria. Later we overheard soldiers talking about that camp. They said it burned to the ground, Sophie."

"Dora, please. Don't fret. It's all true. I was transferred to that camp in Austria, and I stayed there for many weeks. But then I was moved again. I wasn't there the day of the fire. It was all luck, I suppose—or miracle. Besides, I told Michael I would see him again. I had to keep that promise. Right, *zeisele*?" My mother smiled down at me.

"I told her, Mamishu! I told her. I told her just what you said to me. Bobeshi, remember—I said she would be back."

"Yes, darling. Yes, you did. You were perfect. I should have listened to you. It doesn't matter now, though. You see? Look! Your mother is here. She is safe and you will never be apart again."

I felt elation, completion, tenderness, and protection as we glided through the back of the square toward my aunt Cecia's home, hand in hand.

Mamishu said she never thought she would hold her child's hand in hers again. She had prayed—but she had barely believed in God anymore, until this second. She was still a mother. For the first time in a very long while, God had answered one of her prayers.

On the walk to Aunt Cecia's there was so much to talk about.

"I was really sick, Mamishu. You should have seen me. I climbed up on Bobeshi's shoulders and snuck a look inside the infirmary and I saw there weren't any guards. We walked right in the front door after that and climbed into beds—I had my own bed."

I told her how I slept by myself for the very first time and when we woke up there were all kinds of noises outside. "Bobeshi was scared, but I wasn't."

I told Mamishu everything I could remember about our escape to the Auschwitz infirmary and how the whole camp—even the women from our bunk—had to stand in lines. Then everyone marched down the road into the woods until the whole camp was just quiet. I told her about the Soviet troops who made us dress up in our prisoner uniforms again, days after liberation, so they could take our pictures.

Mamishu told us about the camp in Austria where she worked at a munitions factory, just like she had at Pionki. She said she would stand for hours in front of a huge table filled with tiny gun parts. Her job there was to clean the grease off them and prepare them for assembly. Again, her dainty fingers were an asset.

At this place she was treated decently by the SS guards. Conditions were more bearable than they had been at

Auschwitz—but she still worked twelve to fourteen hours a day on her feet.

Then she was selected for work at yet another munitions factory. She didn't know exactly where she was taken, somewhere in the web of Austria's enormous system of concentration camps controlled from a central camp called Mauthausen. She'd been there only a few days, maybe two, when she learned there was a terrible explosion at the first factory where she'd worked. Conditions inside any munitions plant are dangerous, with all the gunpowder and volatile material under one roof. If she had not been moved, she probably would have died—like everyone else inside.

"I thought about you every single, solitary day, Michael," she said. She kept wondering how Bobeshi was faring and if she was able to scrounge enough extra food to keep me nourished. "I should have known you'd stay hidden to the end, my darling." She squeezed my hand as we walked. "You're a survivor."

What seemed to shock my mother the most was the news that Aunt Hilda had returned.

"Oh, yes! She surprised us all," Bobeshi told her.

"At first, I thought she was *you*," I said. I explained I didn't really remember having an aunt named Hilda. "She told me how you used to sing so much when you were both girls that your father, Grandpa Mordecai, would get frustrated and yell, 'I can't hear one more note, Sophie! Sing outside, to the heavens. Hashem (God) will love to hear you but your papa needs a break!'"

My mother giggled. "That's true, *libling*. And guess what? I *still* love to sing!" She paused to think for a second and then broke into song. "I'm back with my sweet Michael . . . never again away. Let's go and let's tell the rest of the fellows . . . Sophie's here to stay!" Mamishu was so blithely silly. One could either find her humor exasperating—or altogether charming. I suspect my father found that light-heartedness to be simply magnetic.

I bet that's why my papa first fell in love with her.

Mamishu continued to hum her tune all the way to Sosnowa Street, where her song, her smile, and her stride all ceased in unison.

Suddenly, my mother started weeping. She covered her face with her hands and sobbed with all her might. I was terrified at the sight. My poor mother!

I didn't understand at first why she was crying. But now I think it was that she had kept her sorrow over my brother's and father's deaths on a shelf, tucked it away for so long, focusing on survival. But seeing our old home up ahead just made it impossible to keep the overwhelming pain at bay.

"Don't be sad, Mamishu. Don't cry," I said.

Then Bobeshi started crying again, too.

I was just a little child and my two protectors were breaking down in front of me. My stomach was in knots as I stood there helpless. My mother and grandmother wept and hugged for a very long time, saying nothing.

I looked down at my hands and realized I was still holding the dandelion chain I'd made on the walk to the square. Without interrupting them, I wordlessly draped the strand of flowers over Mamishu's shoulders until it hung down over her like a scarf.

Mamishu looked at the bright yellow chain I'd made and she smiled. She was still crying, but I knew she liked it. She really liked it.

Minutes more passed while Mamishu and Bobeshi wiped away each other's tears and spoke together softly. Finally, we continued down the street.

But it was another shock to Mami's system when we kept on walking past Bobeshi's and our house and went directly to Aunt Cecia's home, not far away.

"What do you mean someone else is living there? It's our house! Where have you and Michael been living, Dora? Where?"

The conversation about the chicken coop would wait until later. For now, Bobeshi simply explained that a Polish woman had moved to our address and she had no intention of moving out. She said conditions in town were such that arguing to police could not possibly help the situation. "Just let it alone, Sophie. Trust me," Bobeshi said with unwavering conviction. "Michael and I have been doing fine. Let's just go enjoy your reunion with your family, shall we?"

After her emotional release on the street corner, Mamishu had no energy to mourn the loss of her property right now. The three of us continued walking to Aunt Cecia and Uncle Sam's two-story brick house.

Mamishu's heart was beating so fast I could feel the pulse in her thumb, enclosed in my small hand. She was excited to reunite with her brothers and her younger sister.

She turned the handle of the front door without even knocking and leaned her head inside the doorframe. *"A gutn tag?"* she called in Yiddish. Hello?

No one was in the entryway or the parlor. "Sam, Hilda, Mullek?" she called out in a quavering voice.

Silence. No one was home. Disappointed and anxious— the three of us sat down on the couch in the parlor to wait. We didn't wait long.

About five minutes after we arrived, we heard a chorus of familiar voices approaching the porch. Mamishu jumped up from her seat and leaped to the doorway, where from the other side of the glass window in the door, Aunt Hilda gasped loudly. Initially it was a gasp of terror. Someone was inside their home!

The terror instantly turned into joyful shock and amazement.

"Sophie! You're alive?" Aunt Hilda flung open the door to touch her sister's face. "You are back from the dead, my sweet sister?"

Behind Aunt Hilda a parade of siblings and siblings-in-law crowded in to see if it was true.

Moniek said, "We gave up on you, Sophie. We thought we would not see you until the hereafter." He covered his face and bowed his head to try to stop the avalanche of tears. David, too, and Uncle Sam—all burst into tears. Just as I had expected.

My cousin Kristina-Ruth didn't remember Mamishu, of course, but there had been enough surprise reunions in recent weeks that she understood the gravity of this moment.

"Your mami?" Ruth whispered to me.

I nodded proudly.

Mamishu embraced Hilda, hugged the others, and then lifted up my cousin.

"And here is Ruth, you beautiful creature," she said softly. "I've missed you, too, little one. You and Michael must be some troublesome pair these days."

"I know who you are," my cousin said proudly. "Hello, Aunt Sophie! My name, though, is Kristina. Kristina-Ruth Jonisch," she said firmly.

Mamishu looked at Sam and Cecia quizzically.

"We'll explain later," they chortled. "It's a story for another day."

None of it really mattered at this moment. As my aunts and uncles streamed into the house, touching Mamishu's arm or her cheek or squeezing her shoulder to make sure she was real, each carried the weight of unimaginable memories and terrors.

Aunt Hilda would never forget the limp bodies she dragged from the showers at one camp or the bullets she packed, worrying they would one day pierce another Jew's heart.

Ruth carried the agony of being separated from her parents and deposited time and again with strangers.

Sam and Cecia bore the painful scars from having to let Ruth go.

Moniek, Mullek, and David and his wife, Gutia, carried the anxiety of years spent hiding in a dark, windowless attic, wondering if they would ever stroll openly in the sunlight again.

Mamishu, of course, held the terror of learning her son

and her husband had died from a suffocating poison gas inside the chambers at Auschwitz. Bobeshi, too, ached from that knowledge.

On this night, though, all of those agonizing thoughts would be put aside—at least for a time. What we felt on that occasion was God's light.

I sat on Mamishu's lap at dinner, even though I was a little too big for that sort of stuff. Kristina-Ruth sat on her mami's lap because, well, she always did. Aunt Hilda never stopped smiling. Mamishu gently spun the now-wilting chain of golden dandelions between her fingers as she talked and laughed with her siblings.

The company at this table might have looked like a pack of inconsequential diners to anyone peering inside the window. But it was really quite extraordinary. The close-knit Jonisch siblings had parted ways during the war and never expected to be together again, yet here they were. Ruth and I and her cousin Eli and his siblings had made it home, too. It should have been a dinner party with ghosts. But we had all survived.

Thirty-four hundred Jews lived and worked in Żarki before the Holocaust. Less than thirty returned. My family accounted for almost all of them. We were an elite club of survivors, with luck that had conquered all odds.

26

AMERICAN DREAM

"This is where you've been living?" The way Mamishu looked at our chicken coop, we might as well have been inhabiting a hole in the ground. But we had a roof over our heads. There was a well filled with water on the property and a little stream where we could wash our feet and rinse our clothing. Bobeshi had turned empty egg crates upside down for furniture, and the straw we slept on was relatively clean and soft. Animals had not inhabited this coop in years, and the air inside it smelled as crisp as the outdoors. I didn't understand why she was so horrified by our living conditions, but my mother was aghast.

"How could they look me in the face, all of them—laughing over the dinner table and telling me how they loved me so—when they let my child live here like an animal? They're sleeping like kings, each of them with a

bed and blankets and a proper kitchen to share for breakfast in the morning, and Michael is here?"

Mami was red-in-the-face mad.

"Oh, no, Sophie. Don't be angry with them. Cecia and
Sam practically insisted we stay there. David and Moniek
have that apartment in Częstochowa now, even though they
are here every week doing business with Sam. They begged
us to come to Częstochowa, but we are quite comfortable
here. It's so peaceful and serene at night. Michael and I just
sit and talk and listen to the insects play their night songs,
don't we, Michael?"

Bobeshi looked at me.

I knew she was hoping I would say something to dissipate
my mother's obvious frustration. I knew she wanted me to
nod and tell Mamishu how much better it was to be here
living in our chicken coop for the sake of a little privacy.

Oh, was my grandmother ever annoyed when I answered
that I wouldn't mind moving to Kristina's (Ruth's) house.

"Maybe we could just go back there and stay, Mamishu?" I asked.

My mother looked around the coop, perhaps taking note
that there was plenty of space and that it was better than
what we'd had at Auschwitz.

She sighed. "Michael, darling. It's late and it's been a

very long day. Let's all go to sleep and we can revisit this in the morning."

Even as she said this, though, Mamishu continued to glare at my grandmother.

I went outside to relieve myself beside a tree. When I came back in, Mamishu had already snuggled down on a bed of straw, her body slightly curled. I crawled into the space in front of her and felt infinite comfort and security.

I drifted off to sleep, smiling a silly grin.

But as I slipped toward slumber I caught a quiet comment from my mother to Bobeshi that brought me wide awake, although I kept my eyes closed and pretended to sleep.

"He looks like he is two steps from the grave," Mamishu whispered. "Why hasn't his hair grown back? It's been nine months since the boy's head was shaved at Auschwitz!"

My grandmother was answering, but I had covers over my head and her voice was too muffled to hear.

At some point I heard Mamishu say we couldn't stay in Żarki forever. "Dora, there's nothing left here for us."

Whatever Bobeshi said in reply, it must have been a protest, because Mamishu snapped, "No, Dora!"

Staying wasn't an option as far as she was concerned. If we stayed, we'd be no better off than the chickens that should be living where we lay right then. "The gentiles don't want us—most of them hate us. I won't lose another child. I won't!"

I didn't know what my mother was talking about. I felt fine. I had a stubborn rash on my legs and arms, and, yes, my hair wouldn't grow. But I was healthy and strong!

"We're going. It's not a question of *if* but *when*. I'm not asking for your permission, Dora. I'm just inviting you to join us."

I must have drifted off because I don't remember anything else my mother and grandmother said.

In the morning, Bobeshi seemed upset, whereas my mother's sunny mood matched the weather.

"You know, Dora—this little coop has its perks. If we shared a home with my family, that brother Sam of mine would eat every morsel of food we could buy. And he insists on tanning leather in the back room!"

After they'd come out of hiding in Żarki, the Jonisch brothers had taken what gold was left in their secret stashes and purchased animal skins and hides to cure for sale. Business was beginning to percolate. Everyone needed leather for shoes and coats, after all. My uncles had some real money coming in. But Mamishu was scornful that they would even think of starting the business back up.

"Here in this ghost town? And with all those tanning chemicals, it smells like a body is fermenting in chloroform when you walk to the back of their house!" Mamishu quipped. "At least there's fresh air and quiet here. Let's enjoy it while we can, anyway."

"What do you mean?" I asked. "Are we going back to our house on Sosnawa Street?"

"Not exactly," Mamishu said mysteriously. I caught her winking at my grandmother, who wore a face of fury.

"Really, Sophie?" Bobeshi snapped. "You were always a cautious, levelheaded one. Have you lost your mind?"

I didn't know what they were arguing about, but my mother and grandmother spoke in veiled terms with deep sighs of frustration. They were not seeing eye-to-eye about something.

"Let's talk about the future, Dora," Mamishu implored her. My mother tried desperately to convince my grandmother to move to Częstochowa with my uncles. It would only be temporary. Then, she said, we could all travel to America! She said the word "America" the way a child says the word "candy." She told me that America was the most wonderful and welcoming place you can imagine. She said

I could grow up and start my own business there. "If you make money in America, nobody is going to take it from you," she told me. "If you have a house, nobody can push their way inside and steal it from you, Michael." And she promised me there would be more opportunities than I could ever dream about—if we could just find a way to get our sailing papers to the United States.

I've got to hand it to her. My mother could make turpentine soup sound sweet. Her eyes sparkled when she felt passionate about things and—I guess it was the innate survivor in her—when she faced difficulty she found her way back to being happy, no matter what. That's a gift. I think maybe I got a little bit of that from her.

"I'm going to learn how to make hats!" Mamishu said with delight. She ignored Grandma Dora and took both my hands—swinging them out and then in again in front of us as she sang another silly ditty made up on the spot.

I didn't know what she meant by all of this, but her excitement was contagious. "What can I learn to make, Mami?"

"Anything you want, my darling. You can make or do anything you want when we get to America. You want to be a lawyer? You can be one! How about a senator?" She laughed. "First though—school! You're going to work your little tushy off in school, my *libling*. You got a second chance your brother did not get."

It had to have been hard for Mamishu to even mention Samuel. I felt sorry for her when I saw pain wash over her face momentarily. Just like that, though, she defaulted to being happy. "America!"

She told me we would first go to Częstochowa to stay with Uncle David and Uncle Moniek—just for a few months. She could make money helping them with their business. "It will be a pleasure for once, to work hard and actually get paid," she said proudly.

But then came the part of her story I didn't like. She told me Bobeshi would not be coming with us. My heart breaks again just thinking about saying goodbye to the woman who kept me safe inside Auschwitz and brought me back home to Żarki. We shared a bed in a death camp, and now in a Żarki chicken coop we shared a mattress of straw.

No begging from my mother or from me would change Bobeshi's mind, though.

"You need to go with your mother now, *libling*. I am too old for more adventure, Michael. I'm all out of energy for new journeys—and you are both fresh and ready for a new life." My grandmother was resolute. "There's no point in hounding me this time, darling. Żarki is my home, and this is where I stay."

27

AT A CROSSROADS

A few days later, we were all at Uncle Sam and Aunt Cecia's house for a lunch of brisket, sauerkraut, and a little rhubarb cake. They told me it was a celebratory lunch for my fifth birthday, which had long since come and gone, and they sang to me in Polish, Yiddish, and Hebrew. Other than that, it was an ordinary lunch until my family began to contemplate and plan a new future.

We had survived the Holocaust. But now what? It was finally time for my mother to make her case. The war was over in Europe, but in Żarki there was no life left for a Jew to live. Everywhere my relatives went they were made to feel shut out. Despite the people who welcomed my family's return, some people in Żarki seemed simply agitated by our presence.

Mamishu launched into her campaign to get the family

to go to America. They could finally do what they now realized they should have done before the war: they could leave.

With the exception of Bobeshi, all of my relatives had already been dreaming of the very same plan. My uncles said they first needed to tie up loose ends. They had already begun to plant roots for their leather business, and they would have to unload some merchandise and materials.

"I'll help!" Mamishu exclaimed, before they could even ask.

"Well, yes, of course you will, Sophie. We will need all hands on deck, darling. You and Michael will stay with David and me in the apartment in Częstochowa. You will carry samples to merchants and scout out sales," Moniek said, reading Mamishu's mind.

"Yes, that would be wonderful!" Mamishu trilled.

I thought it would be wonderful, too. Mamishu and I were starting an adventure together. Oh, and Aunt Hilda would be joining us. We would all stay in Częstochowa, where my family would collectively try to turn a small stock of leather goods into a jackpot to begin anew.

Częstochowa was less than a sixty-minute carriage ride away, so we could visit Żarki often.

That night, we returned to the chicken coop, and Mamishu packed what little we had in a satchel for the trip the next day. Very early the next morning, we left in a wagon alongside Aunt Hilda. Bobeshi stood along the side of the road, waving to us—to me—until she was just a tiny speck in the distance.

The air was moist, and dew clung to the leaves all along the wooded path. When a low branch would brush against the wagon, we were sprinkled with a cool mist. We rode mostly in silence, our voices not yet fully awake. Finally, the road opened up and we could see Częstochowa ahead.

To me, it looked like a large city. I had heard about it often from my aunts and uncles and even from my cousin Ruth, who had stayed in the orphanage there during the war. Like Żarki, Częstochowa had been decimated by bombing and Nazi carnage. The town's own Bloody Monday would be remembered in the history books. But unlike in Żarki, where only twenty-seven Jews remained after the war, Częstochowa had become a meeting place for survivors in the region. There were more than thirteen hundred Jews registered in the city when we arrived. There were many more passing through, and most people were hoping for a Jewish revival, right there, in the middle of Poland.

My family had all but given up on that. We just wanted to settle ourselves long enough to gather money for America.

"Well, here you are," the carriage driver said as he dropped us in front of my uncles' gray concrete apartment building. We didn't have to pay him. David and Moniek had already taken care of that.

The pair of brothers appeared on the street in front of the building to greet us.

"Welcome, dear sisters!" David said as he leaned way down to kiss Mamishu and Aunt Hilda on both sides of their cheeks. David was the tallest of the Jonisch brothers, by far. "And hello to you, young man," he said as he reached out to shake my hand. We walked up to the second floor of the building, where my uncles' three-room apartment looked like an animal collector's lair. Everywhere, animal skins and leather scraps were draped over tables and chairs. The open windows let in a light breeze, but it did nothing to cover the pungent smell of tanning chemicals.

"Ewwww!" I held my nose and stifled a cough. Mamishu and Aunt Hilda gave their brothers a disapproving look, but what could they say, really? David and Moniek were providing them with shelter and opportunity. And my uncles, not fathers themselves, didn't even think to worry how the chemical fumes might affect a small child.

Food tends to make everything better—especially for people who know to appreciate every morsel—so after a heavy lunch of beef stew and beet salad, the smell seemed more tolerable. The grown-ups began to talk again about the future, while I napped on the couch, still tired from the early-morning journey.

I don't remember much about my stay in Częstochowa except that I can say with certainty that as the weeks went by, I grew stronger and healthier. My hair started to grow back, fell out again, and then grew back once more. My body was fighting. My stomach was definitely filling out, and so were my legs and my arms, which stuck out awkwardly at the ends of my shirts and pants—all of which I had outgrown. Mamishu and Aunt Hilda had grown, too—their arms and legs were meatier, and their hips were now soft and curved the way they should be. Aunt Hilda had broken a tooth in one of the camps, and she now had the money to have it repaired. Her skin was healthy, and both women's hair had grown thicker and more luxurious.

Aunt Hilda knew a lot about math and accounting, so she tended to my schooling when she could. Both she and Mamishu alternately watched over me, and helped their brothers with the business. I went from having no mother at all to having what felt like two mothers in the span of a very short time.

I don't know exactly how long we stayed in Częstochowa, with its relatively busy merchant squares and active parlors, but after what was probably about six months, a letter found its way to Aunt Hilda from overseas. It was from the eldest Jonisch sibling, Ola. She and her family had traveled across all of Russia and Siberia and finally made it to Japan a year and a half after the war had started—saved, really, by a famous Japanese diplomat named Chiune Sugihara. The courageous statesman had provided visas for some six thousand Jews during the war, against his own government's wishes.

Now Ola wanted to arrange for Hilda to escape Poland, too. Ola, highly intellectual and fiercely protective of her youngest sibling, was instructing Hilda to travel to Sweden, where she would then board a boat for Cuba. It was, Ola believed, the quickest route to a better life.

"Come with me, Sophie!" Hilda begged as she tucked the postcard from Ola into her dress pocket. "You and Michael and me! We will travel to Cuba. And from there—to America!"

Mamishu had different plans in mind.

She had been talking about going to Munich, Germany, to get our travel papers to America. "There are all kinds of services there," she told her brothers and Hilda. "There's an occupational training group that can teach us trades so we can get work. There are schools where Michael will be welcomed and accepted. He can study Hebrew! Mostly, though, we need to get Michael to a good doctor. I need to get him well above anything else."

Our new destination must have sounded confusing to me.

"Germany" was a word that had gone hand-in-hand with "evil" for so many years. It is hard to understand how a country that had waged war against us could—within months—have become a place where we might find peace and protection.

Mamishu explained that the Allies were rebuilding Munich, which had been destroyed in the war. Many relief organizations stood ready to help us there. They were already on the ground finding jobs and housing for people displaced by the war.

That was it. The time had come for the sisters to part again and hope their paths would merge again someday.

Before they both bid farewell to Poland, we all returned one more time to Żarki for a visit with Sam, Cecia, Mullek, and of course Bobeshi. It was a bittersweet parting for us, my grandmother and me—this time, it felt so very permanent.

I sat next to her in Cecia's dining room and held

Bobeshi's hand under the table the whole evening. At the end of the meal, the men stood in the parlor and prayed while I helped my aunts and my mother clear the table. I saw Mamishu lean in to say something in my grandmother's ear as they put away jars in the cupboard.

"*Sha!*" said Bobeshi, trying to convince my mother out of whatever she was planning.

It was no use.

Mamishu untied her apron and set it on the countertop. "I just need to tend to one little task before Michael and I can leave Poland," my mother said aloud to my aunt Hilda, who winked at her.

"Yes, go on, Sophie. We'll be here waiting," Hilda said.

I didn't learn until much later what my mother did next.

28

ALL THAT REMAINED

Mamishu threw a coat over her shoulders and stepped into the cold night air. She scurried down the street, her footsteps light and quick. She was racing straight back to her old house.

It didn't even look like her house anymore. Five years of wartime depression had left their mark. The paint on the wood trim around the windows was rough and worn, the front door looked like it could fall right from its hinges, and the windowpanes themselves were covered in grime.

All the better for me now! Mamishu must have thought as she tiptoed silently along the ten-foot gap between her old home and her neighbor's house.

Her heart was racing, but she had no intention of turning around—not until she found what she had come for. The spirited, indelicate side of my mother was pulling her to march up to the back door and start banging—ready to face off with the woman who had stolen her home. Fortunately, the practical side of her brain kept her moving silently down the narrow path toward her goal.

My mother stepped to the edge of the back porch and began to count. *Eyn, tsvey, dray, fir,* she recited silently in her head as she took each carefully measured step.

When her husband first buried the family's stash of money and jewels, it had been pretty easy to spot its location, if you knew where to look.

Five years later, Mamishu had to rely on rough measurements.

Did Israel say thirteen steps, or was it fourteen?

Mamishu was second-guessing herself. She paced out her steps several times, eyeing the distance from the house and the distance to the neighbor's yard, trying to remember exactly where everything was in relation to that spot.

Knowing that her family was undoubtedly racked with worry, she finally dropped to her knees to dig. She dug into the earth with just her hands. Suddenly, a sharp needling of pain shot from her index finger, jolting her to howl out loud. Her fingernails were so weak from malnourishment that one had nearly snapped backward, ripping from her skin.

Mamishu wrapped the fingers from her other hand tight

around the fingertip to stop the bleeding. She felt so much pain from that one small fingertip. There wasn't time to think about it, though.

She forced her brain to turn that sharp ache into a dull numbness—the same way she anesthetized her agony in Auschwitz and countless other situations. My mother just kept on digging and, after a while, even though her raw fingertip still bled, she felt no pain.

She hadn't noticed that a light had come on inside the house next door.

She dug deeper, cupping palmfuls of soil in her hands and tossing it away.

Finally, she felt something foreign peeking out of the earth. The moon provided just enough light for her to see—it was a burlap sack, inside the makeshift vault Papa had fashioned.

We're saved.

My mother knew that Papa had left enough zlotys in the bag to get set up in a new city. Surely the crystal vase, the assorted pieces of gold, the string of pearls, and other valuables in the sack would net a nice amount of money for my schooling and some proper clothes.

Infused with energy, she kept digging and pulled at the top edge of the bag until she wrested it free from the ground. With that final pull, it flew into the air.

Why does the bag feel so light?

Mamishu's face flushed. She knew before she reached into the burlap sack what had happened. She had been robbed again.

She imagined herself finding a large rock in the yard and hurling it at the kitchen window of her old home. She pictured herself banging on the back door like a lunatic, screaming *Thieves! You are heartless thieves!*

But my mother realized quickly that the person who inhabited her home now might not have been the same one who stole our family treasures. Nazi soldiers and local vandals had tramped through yards and basements in search of hidden treasure even before every Jew was expelled from Żarki. Surely, such activity had continued long after the Jews were gone.

We should have buried it under the foundation of the house!

Her safety net was gone, along with every last physical memory of her old life with my papa.

Another piece of my mother's heart felt utterly broken. She was about to toss the sack to the ground and leave, defeated, when she noticed something. There was still some small weight inside the bag. It was dark out, but her sense of touch was heightened after thirty minutes of working without light.

She reached into the bottom of the sack and felt

something cool and curved. A skinny stem, a wide opening at the top—she knew just what this was. In all honesty, at that moment she would have preferred the gold coins. She indulged in one brief second of desperate self-pity. But it took her just seconds more to realize that what she held in that bag carried more value than any pile of banknotes or any precious jewels.

She carefully reached her other arm into the sack and pulled out our family's silver kiddush cup.

Any gentile thief or Nazi thug would have considered the Jewish artifact trash. To Mamishu, this was the greatest treasure of all. Hitler's army had killed millions of Jews, but it was abundantly clear on that night: you can kill people, but you can't destroy faith.

With memories of Shabbat dinners and laughter swirling in her mind, Mamishu returned the cup to the bag and clutched it to her heart as she started back to the side of the house with a victorious smile on her face. The money could be replaced; her brothers would see to it that she had enough to get to Munich. The family kiddush cup, though, was irreplaceable.

But as she rounded the corner to the front of the house, she heard a loud *click*. A split second later, she was face-to-face with the barrel of a pistol.

29

BACKYARD ENCOUNTER

"I've caught you, you swine!" said the man whose pistol was now cocked and pointed at Mamishu's face. "What do you have there?" He nodded down toward the sack at her chest.

Beg him to spare your life! Rip the gun from his hands. Run!

My mother had dodged and deceived death so many times—in Żarki on Bloody Monday, at the selection gate at Auschwitz, at the labor camp in Austria. She had traveled hundreds of miles and back to Żarki to reunite with a son who had cheated death, too. And here, in her own backyard, she could very well die at the hands of her own countryman.

"Answer me quick, woman! I've got three bullets in my clip but I'll only need one to end your life."

But Mamishu couldn't speak. She tilted her head an

inch, trying to force full motion back into her body. That little tilt of her neck allowed moonlight to brighten her profile—just enough.

"Sophie?" the man said. "Sophie Bornstein?"

Mamishu didn't answer. She couldn't. Her face must have registered that she was indeed Sophie Bornstein, though.

"Sophie, it's me. You remember? Lukasz Baros."

She did remember. The year before the war, her accountant husband had helped Lukasz out of a big mess with his finances, some complication with his farm and the bank. She also remembered that he had come to their house late at night because, well, it wouldn't have been proper for him to be seen working with a Jew.

"You made it back, eh?" Lukasz said. Then he realized he was still holding the pistol, pointed in Mamishu's direction. He put it away and apologized. "Sophie, I would never have pulled my gun if I'd realized it was you. I just thought it was some wandering refugee looking for easy loot."

Finally, words and movement slipped back into Mamishu's body. "Lukasz, this is my house. You remember that, too, don't you? I've just come for some things Israel left behind. There's nothing here really," she said. "Empty bag."

Lukasz seemed harmless now, and she no longer feared for her life. She still worried he might take her kiddush cup, if only to melt it down for the silver.

Lukasz was shaking his head. "So few of your people returned, Sophie. Houses around this neighborhood were empty for so long after you left that some of us figured we'd move in to care for the houses and keep this area orderly. I've had this house for about two years," he said nodding to our next-door neighbor's home.

"I was just looking out for Issa Olkowski," he said, nodding toward my mother's old home. "Things have been tough around here ever since the war—for all of us. We keep an eye out for one another. I am sorry that your place is occupied now, Sophie." Then he added with the hint of a question in his voice, "Tell Israel I say hello? Right?"

"Sure, I will, Lukasz. Be well." Mamishu did not wish to prolong this conversation. She also didn't care to share any of her life, her heartbreak, with this man.

She just wanted to get back to the family, return to Częstochowa, and pack her bags one more time to leave the country forever. She wanted to climb aboard a train with me by her side. She wanted to stare out the train car window watching Poland's landscape grow distant, daydreaming about celebrating the Sabbath in America. One day she would raise her kiddush cup filled with sweet wine.

The future seemed clear to her. She did not realize the quiet hum of socially accepted anti-Semitism would still present one last, terrifying hurdle—for me.

30

CITY OF RUBBLE

I swallowed hard, despite the acorn-sized lump in my throat, and waved goodbye to my grandmother and my aunt Hilda at the train station in Częstochowa. We'd said goodbye to my busy uncles earlier in the day. Bobeshi didn't like to travel outside Żarki, but she agreed to take a carriage ride to the city to see us off.

"Here you are, *zeisele*," she said stoically as she handed me a fragrant paper sack. "You'll open it on the train. Be safe in Germany. I'll be safe here."

She was short on words and drama, as usual. I wanted to jump into her arms for a giant hug. I wanted to change her mind about coming with us to Munich. She was "serious" Bobeshi, though. She simply wanted to wish us well.

Aunt Hilda came for just the opposite. She kissed me all over my cheeks and chin and nose. *Mwah, mwah, mwah . . .*

She made the sound for kissing as she showered me with farewell affection.

"Chicken soup and *lokshen* for lunch in America, shall we say, ten years from now?" Hilda asked as she turned to her big sister.

"Well, of course, *meyne lib*—my darling," Mamishu said.

Just as their mother, Esther, had preached, they promised to always look forward. Hilda would be traveling soon to Sweden and then to Cuba. She hoped that from there, America would be the final stop.

"So? We should go?" Mamishu looked at me to signal it was time. I climbed onto the train platform and waved goodbye to my aunt and my grandmother, hoping and expecting I would see them again in my life.

"*Shalom, zeisele,*" I saw Bobeshi mouth to me. *Shalom* is a Hebrew word that has three meanings: "hello," "goodbye," and "peace." I hoped she meant the latter. It was too hard to think she was saying goodbye forever. She was, though. That was the last time I would see my grandmother. We never returned to Żarki in her lifetime, and to the best of my knowledge, she never left.

"Can I open my gift from Bobeshi?" I asked as soon as I had planted myself on an empty bench on the train.

"If your grandmother said it was all right."

I ripped open the paper sack and smiled a huge, silly grin. Two dozen red, plump, perfect wild strawberries.

As hard as it was to think about being so far from Bobeshi, I know I was excited to go to Munich.

Mamishu had packed another bag filled with nuts and wild honey and other fortifying snacks, and she carried a satchel with all of our belongings: three pairs of trousers, two shirts, and five pairs of socks and underwear for me; undergarments, a hat, and one cotton floral dress, hand-sewn by Aunt Cecia, for her. There was also one silver kiddush cup.

My mother and I traveled all day, first south to Krakow and then west into Czechoslovakia. Finally, we transferred to a train that would take us to Munich.

By the time we arrived, it was late evening and I had fallen asleep with my head pressed against the side of Mamishu's arm. She wiggled me awake and I climbed onto my knees to peer outside the window as the train pulled to a stop at the station in Munich. The way Mamishu had talked about this place, I had expected more. Maybe she did, too. Neither of us spoke. We just climbed down from the train platform and followed signs to one of the main squares nearby.

We were headed to a small displaced persons (DP) camp inside the city. Mamishu had been in contact with the Hebrew Immigrant Aid Society (HIAS), which along with other refugee relief agencies was working to help get survivors back on their feet after the war. The DP camp would be expecting us. It was in an American-held zone of Munich.

To get there, though, we had to navigate through dark streets and alleys where twenty-foot-tall piles of concrete and brick rubble nearly blocked the entire path. The markings of war were still very present in Munich. It wasn't the capital city of Germany, but it had been the center of Nazi power and thus had been a prime target for the Allied forces. The Allies carpet-bombed Munich relentlessly from the air, destroying centuries of neoclassical and renaissance architecture. Most of the city's treasured buildings had been taken over by Nazis at the start of the war. The Gestapo had turned the palace where Bavarian kings once lived into a prison; like so many other majestic sites, it had been destroyed in aerial attacks.

Even late at night, you could hear work crews' clanging machinery—the mighty sounds of progress in a city struggling to recover. There was not one street we passed that didn't have buildings with visible damage. Some were inhabitable; many others were eerily vacant.

Then there was that other sound.

"Es wird spät. Werden wir jetzt nach Hause gehen?"

It was just casual conversation among locals strolling by. But it was in German—a language that my brain now equated with Auschwitz. I heard the language and I instantly heard the sound of polished leather boots marching, even when they weren't there. I shuddered and, more than once, nervously peered over my shoulder expecting to see an SS guard. I didn't ask her, but I suspect Mamishu experienced the same thing. We hadn't heard German since the Nazis fled Poland many months earlier.

Mamishu unfolded a city map as we maneuvered through Munich's streets. "Aha!" she exclaimed, pointing to a building with a banner that had the name of the camp. It was administered by the United Nations Relief and Rehabilitation Administration. An American flag had been draped over a high stone ledge by the doorway. This was definitely the place a homeless immigrant would go for refuge.

The camp was really a cluster of maybe four or five multistory concrete buildings. We walked inside what appeared to be the main office, and instantly heard commotion. It was strange, given the late hour. Women milled about in nightgowns and coats, and everyone looked nervous. There were several clusters of people talking anxiously, some weeping. Behind the wooden table at the front of the room, workers also stood in groups talking in soft tones but wildly waving their arms in panic.

"She's been crying for five straight days. Someone should have been with her at all times!" I heard one worker say.

"I knew she was struggling, but I never imagined she would do something so drastic," the other one said.

There were women soothing tearful children who clearly had a better handle on what was happening than I did. Mamishu was trying to cover my ears and shield me so I couldn't follow the conversations. Minutes later, we heard a siren outside.

A very nice aid worker spotted us in the corner of the room where Mamishu was trying to keep me out of the way of the bustle. She came over and introduced herself as Talia. Then she pulled us into an intake room and got us registered.

Talia didn't say anything about the chaos in the lobby or what had happened just outside one of the buildings that prompted ambulance and police sirens. She simply marked down some of our information, told us where we would be sleeping, and hurried us along to our room. She told us we should feel at home.

When we finally slipped under the sheets of our cot in a

large space filled with other refugees sleeping on lined-up steel-frame beds, our roommates whirred with tragic gossip.

"She just didn't want to live without her husband and children. She told me so, again and again. I should have known."

"Honestly, Irit—I would do the very same thing if I had the courage. Right now, Golda is hugging her babies up in heaven. Where am I? Here on this disappointing earth without a single member of my family remaining!"

"Stop it, Shoshanah! You're horrid for thinking such fatalistic things. Tell me you didn't survive two years of torture and humiliation in a death camp just so you could take your life yourself? You were gifted with a second chance! You'd prefer to dive off a building and throw it away?" said a woman wearing a blue-striped nightdress that must have been a hand-me-down. Her large breasts spilled out the front of the scoop-neck gown.

The woman named Shoshanah laughed. "Well, I didn't say I'd dive off a building! I'd jump off a bridge, maybe, into a nice shallow river. Or perhaps I'd take a bottle filled with sleeping pills. That's a far more comfortable way to go," she said with a wicked smile.

My mother didn't find anything amusing about this

conversation. She later said she realized that night that she had more to worry about than just earning money and gaining travel visas. She would worry from then on that depression could sneak up on us. We had both witnessed so much horror.

As we fell asleep, she murmured a tune in my ear that sounded familiar. "This is not your last journey. Don't say this is your last path . . ."

It was not the end of our journey. It was just the beginning. But here's the problem. It was not the end of our heartache either. Plenty of people still hated Jews in Germany—and I would soon be reminded of that terrible, awful fact.

31

THE DARK SIDE OF MUNICH

Despite our rough first night, the DP camp was not a bad place. There were always clean sheets and water for washing our clothes and taking baths. There was a cafeteria where hundreds of people enjoyed free meals and snacks.

I ate voraciously. My relationship with food was fast becoming a tumultuous one. When I saw bowls of fruit or packages of snacks set out on countertops around camp or in the cafeteria, I could not leave them sitting there. I ate until my stomach ached some days.

Mamishu was more focused on schooling than on nutrition. She signed me up for classes offered at the DP camp, and she reviewed her own choices for education. The options were overwhelming. One agency that helped place Jews in jobs could train her to do anything, from running movie reels in cinemas to making dresses. In the end, she stuck with her original plan to learn hat making. One week later, she began turning wool swatches, lines of ribbon, and colorful feathers into magnificent pieces.

Every day, she left for training early and I joined packs of other refugee children in a large auditorium-type room where we were grouped by age and language to begin our education. One thing most of our parents agreed on was that education would be our ticket to somewhere better. I didn't hate my classes and Mamishu didn't hate the camp, but she was anxious to gain independence.

Once again, I must admit that dates and times are hard to remember. To a six-year-old boy, three days can feel like three months and vice versa. So I can't say exactly how long we stayed at the DP camp in Munich, but I know that Mamishu was elated when she learned we would be getting our own home. The HIAS office in Munich assisted my mother in securing a one-room apartment on the second floor of a run-down building, not far from the center of the city. HIAS made all the arrangements and covered the deposit and the first month's rent.

"It's all ours!" Mamishu said, beaming, as we set down our little collection of things. We had let ourselves into the building on Agnes Strasse, and this was our first glimpse of the place. There was a small cot in the corner of the room and a brown couch with frayed upholstery. That's where I would sleep—on my very own couch.

HIAS had cosigned the lease, and we had picked up the keys from the agency's headquarters without meeting the landlady. I can't say that Mamishu would have turned down the opportunity had she met the landlady first—but she certainly would have signed the lease with some hesitation.

"I've just come to say hello and let you know I'll be downstairs if you need anything," said the woman who knocked at our door a few minutes after we'd set down our things. She introduced herself as Renée Müller.

Mamishu gasped. The landlady was a slim creature with a sharp, angled nose and a stern expression. Her hair was cut neatly in a dark brown bob, and her outfit was a cheerless beige skirt ensemble. But it was not her severe appearance that caused Mamishu to gasp aloud; it was her necklace: hanging from a gold chain around her neck was a thick gold swastika. The Nazi symbol was as familiar to my mother and me as the moon at night. Anyone who displayed it was unmistakably sending the message *I hate Jews.*

Frau Müller caught my mother's glance at her necklace but offered no apology. She fingered the sharp edges of the gold emblem carefully. "Well, like I said, I'll be watching out for you."

"Of course, how gracious of you, Frau Müller. *Danke schön*—thank you," Mamishu said in carefully pronounced German, and did her best to smile before closing and locking the door.

There was no kitchen in our apartment. We had been told by HIAS that our landlady offered tenants the use of her kitchen.

"Well," Mamishu said aloud, "we shall have lots of picnics in this apartment!" Then she smiled wide. "Let's get some rags, and you can help me clean the windows in our new home, Michael."

It was inconceivable to think that Frau Müller would want to have two immigrant Jews sharing her space. Why had she even rented to a Jew? My mother had no idea.

For a split second she must have considered running right out of there. Uncle Sam, Aunt Cecia, and Ruth had just arrived in Munich and had gone straight into an apartment with money saved from the leather business. They were living about five kilometers away; surely they would take us in. But like always, my mother intended to make the best of a bad situation. We would stay.

In the morning, Mamishu took my hand and led me up the street to where I would be enrolled in a Hebrew gymnasium. That's a special school where teachers speak only

Hebrew from morning until afternoon. It sounded like a punishment to me. I knew a little Hebrew—but Yiddish, Polish, and now even German came more naturally to me. I begged Mamishu not to send me there.

"I'll look so dumb! I won't understand anything, Mamishu! And everyone will laugh at me!" I said as she pulled me by my hand toward the steps of the school.

"Michael, darling"—I knew she wouldn't listen—"you are my brilliant little boy. You'll learn quickly. And then, how wonderful! We can speak together in Hebrew. Your papa would have been so proud to see you entering these doors."

I was worried about school, but I was also worried about my stupid hair—it still wouldn't grow back thick and nice. We had seen a doctor shortly after we arrived in Munich, and he said I had suffered a severe vitamin deficiency, prompting an illness called scurvy. I was eating well now and taking special medicine, but my body hadn't quite caught up.

Mamishu, once the most tenderhearted woman, was so focused on getting us to America now that she had no time for empathy. She just kissed my cheek, straightened my shirt collar, and prodded me on my way. "You're going to be fine, little one. You look so handsome!"

We walked in through a grand, oversized doorway, and I was intimidated by the large hallway. Munich's Hebrew gymnasium was enormous! A large number of Jews had resettled in the area, and many hoped to emigrate to Palestine. Learning Hebrew was a top priority. I still didn't understand why I needed to learn it, though, since we planned to go to America.

Mamishu was wildly impressed by the building. When we entered the office of the headmaster, she threw her shoulders back and proudly spoke in fluent Hebrew—announcing that I would be a wonderful new addition to the school. I was going, like it or not.

When we returned home to our apartment, Frau Müller was there sitting on the porch. She had been there in the morning, too, watching us go. She said very little. She just stared and nodded as we inched past her.

Two days later, on my very first morning of school, we left home earlier than usual. Mamishu had a training class herself through the agency, and she needed to get me on my way.

We rushed down the narrow staircase in the apartment and out the door. Sure enough, Frau Müller was there on the stoop, waiting.

"*Entschuldigen*—excuse me," Mamishu said. "I'm so clumsy. We're in a bit of a rush this morning."

Frau Müller seemed to just glare at us. That's how it felt, anyway. We tried to ignore her as best as we could.

"Mami, please, why can't you just take me to the front door of the school?" I pleaded.

"Michael, we are both students now. Look, *libling*." Mamishu pointed down the street. "Your school is just a few blocks away. I've got to get to my class. It starts in five minutes."

Then she ducked her head under the brim of my gray wool cap to kiss my cheeks and she breezed out of sight. I was left alone to walk the rest of the way to school. It wasn't far. I walked as quickly as I could. But just a few hundred yards before I reached the gymnasium—when it was clear I was headed to the Jewish school—two boys approached. They were maybe twelve years old and they jogged toward me shouting, *"Jude!"* They took turns shoving me back and I stumbled to stay on my feet.

"Shouldn't we be cleaning our armpits with soap made from your fat, instead of seeing you walk our streets?" one of the boys taunted. Then the other stole my cap. That felt worse than any punch or blow could feel—knowing my ugly scalp was exposed. They looked at my fuzzy head of thin, broken hair and I won't ever forget how wickedly they laughed, pointing at me and shouting insults.

That scene repeated itself many times on the streets of

Munich. I never knew when I might run into trouble. Even a year later, after my hair grew in, I was bullied because I had gained so much weight. Whenever I opened my mouth to speak, my Yiddish accent betrayed my religion. It seemed a German kid was often there to remind me that I was nothing.

But it would be an adult who dealt the most permanent blow, when I was least expecting it.

32

THE LADY WITH THE SWASTIKA NECKLACE

Sometimes Mamishu left the house alone to do "secret work." She was dealing on the black market, buying American luxuries like cigarettes and hosiery from U.S. soldiers who patrolled the streets in Munich and then selling the items to local stores. To avoid being caught, she would have to stand for a long time, pretending to shop in the stores, until there were no customers in sight.

She often worked late into the night. I worried that she would be arrested and I would be separated from her again. I cried myself to sleep almost every single evening that she worked.

Sometimes, when my mother knew that she would be out late, she would send me to Uncle Sam and Aunt Cecia's apartment. It was too far to walk there, so I would hitchhike with Mami's help. I did this often. I much preferred to be with my relatives than home by myself worrying about Mamishu.

"I have to go away for the day. I may be very late," my mother said to me one morning in the spring of 1948. I was eight years old. It was a bright, sunny day in Munich and I was disappointed not to be spending it with Mamishu.

I put on a sour face and whined, "May I at least go and play at Ruth's place?"

"I was just going to suggest that, darling. Yes, you'll spend the day with them, and you may sleep there. I'll come for you in the morning very early, before school."

I instantly ran to the closet where my overnight sack was packed for such occasions. I only needed to throw in my toothbrush and I was ready to go.

Mamishu walked me downstairs to help me hail a ride.

"*Entschuldigen*, Frau Müller," mother said as we passed by the stoop.

The landlady just nodded and stared like she always did.

There was pretty regular traffic near our apartment building on Agnes Strasse, and it didn't take Mamishu long to find me a ride. An open-topped vehicle, like some variety of jeep, pulled to the side of the road.

"Need a ride?" asked the friendly German in the driver's seat. He was about my mother's age and had unremarkable features—brown hair, brown eyes, a slim mustache with a divot cut down the center, as was the style then. Mamishu seemed pleased with herself that she had found a ride so quickly. She had places to be.

"That would be wonderful, yes!" Mamishu walked me around to the passenger side of the man's vehicle and helped me climb inside. "Just the little one, today. This is my son, Michael. He's trying to get to his aunt and uncle's home." She explained where Uncle Sam and Aunt Cecia lived and asked the man if it would be inconvenient for him to take me straight there.

"Not at all," said the man. *"Jude?"* he asked—more curiously than spitefully.

"Yes. We are Jewish," said my mother without any hint of apology. "I trust you don't mind?"

"Of course not." The man grinned at me. "I'll take care of . . . Michael? Don't worry. It's quite a nice day for a drive. You're doing me a favor taking me out of my way."

It was a beautiful day. As we drove along the bumpy Munich streets, hitting potholes and dodging construction work, we started to turn a direction I didn't recognize.

"Didn't my mother tell you the way?" I asked with some concern. That internal alarm we all have inside our guts was suddenly sounding. "This doesn't seem right," I said more quietly than I should have.

The man just ignored me and kept driving. I thought

about jumping out of the top of the vehicle and running at full speed. He had a trailer of some kind attached to the back of his jeep and I could have hopped onto it and scooted off the end. But I didn't.

Finally, he spoke. "How old are you?"

I didn't answer.

The man slowly tapped on his brakes and pulled the car cautiously to the side of the road in a quiet neighborhood. I was paralyzed with fear—my intuition telling me to run, but my body ignoring the call. The man looked around to see that there was no one walking along the road. It was broad daylight, but no one was in sight. Then he reached for me.

This man who had seemed so cheerful and kind as he chatted with my mother only minutes earlier set out to assault me. I didn't scream or yell—I felt helpless. The details of the incident aren't something I choose to talk about, even here when I have finally committed to telling my story. I was lucky, really, that I got away at all. As soon as I was able, I grabbed for the door handle and pulled it down with all my might, sending the jeep door swinging open. I tumbled onto the ground facefirst, but there was no time to lie there reeling. I scurried quickly to my feet, the door to the man's open-top vehicle still wide open. He didn't run after me, but I still sprinted with all my strength until I couldn't run anymore. The man was long gone.

I paused for a moment to get my bearings and catch my breath. We hadn't traveled far—only far enough to turn down a quiet street I didn't recognize. I still could find my way back to 64 Agnes Strasse. I was desperate to fall into Mamishu's arms and let her comfort me. I knew she wouldn't be home, of course. I would wait in the apartment with the lights on all night until she arrived.

But as I approached the apartment, I should have guessed—there was Frau Müller, our landlady with the swastika necklace. How I hated that necklace! I tried to shuffle past Frau Müller, who, as always, was blocking my path.

She stopped me gently. "Would you like to come and sit with me?" she asked. "We will wait for your mother together. She comes and goes when she is working, you know. And I believe she will be back shortly."

There was a tiny space on the stoop next to her, and she inched over even farther to create more room. I settled into that spot and sat with Frau Müller for what may have been hours. I knew I must have been crying when I approached the apartment and I intermittently cried as I sat there. I tried not to think about what had happened to me. I knew when my mother got home she would be heartbroken and upset. But then she would say, *"Gam ze ya'avor."* She would tell me that tomorrow would be a new day. This too shall pass. I knew inside it was true. In fact, right there in front of me, on the same day when I saw evil—I saw grace.

Frau Müller put her arm around me and just let me cry in silence, my head leaned against her shoulder, just inches away from where her swastika necklace hung. She got up only a few times—and that was to bring me snacks from her own apartment or to refill a cup of lemonade.

When she finally returned, Mamishu was stunned to find me there on the stoop with our landlady. She pulled me into her arms and looked to Frau Müller for explanation.

Frau Müller only said, "Michael has had a very bad day. Why don't you get cleaned up and then, please, come by the kitchen. I'll prepare some supper for you both."

Upstairs in our one-room apartment, I told my mother what had happened to me. Just as expected, she was devastated and also furious. But it was no use going to the police, she said. The man was probably long gone. We had no way to identify him and no way to prove the crime. But I would never hitchhike again.

That's not the only thing that changed after that day.

We learned to be more cautious—but we also learned that people aren't always what they seem. Sometimes they're worse. Sometimes they're a lot better. And sometimes they're just conflicted.

After that, Frau Müller stayed with me often and allowed me inside her apartment so that I wasn't always alone in the evenings. Her grown daughter gave me piano lessons on the old upright Bechstein piano in their home. Sometimes our landlady walked me to school or cooked us meals; often she and Mamishu would talk and laugh over tea in her kitchen.

I also never again questioned why Mamishu insisted I make school my top priority, and why she prioritized her own work and studies. We would do what we had to do so that a trip to America would be possible. I was never able to easily speak Hebrew (a language I found infinitely difficult), but I understood it well enough to quickly score perfect marks at the gymnasium.

By late 1948, almost all of my aunts and uncles were in Munich—all of us waiting for visas to America. Uncle David and Uncle Moniek left their apartment and their business behind in Częstochowa. They started up again in

Munich while they waited to gain entry to America. Surviving members of the Zborowski family, Kristina-Ruth's cousins and our neighbors in Żarki, had moved to Germany, too. Uncle Mullek had also now arrived in Munich.

We took turns celebrating holidays at one another's apartments—my mother always unwrapping our family's kiddush cup for these occasions.

One Sabbath, we even invited Frau Müller to join us for the holiday feast. She declined. I guess that was a bridge too far for her. Mamishu counted her among her close friends, though, and Frau Müller shared with us what her heart would allow. She shared her kitchen and her conversation, but I don't remember her ever being comfortable traveling out in public with us. She still wore her swastika charm, but she tucked it under her shirt before she knocked on our door to collect rent or to visit.

Sometimes she visited with packages that arrived at the apartment while we were out. The most exciting kind of mail came from an organization called the Cooperative for American Remittances to Europe (CARE). If people think small donations to organizations like this are meaningless, then I am here to report that when we opened boxes from CARE, Mamishu and I practically danced around the living room—holding up chocolates and jars of cherry hard candies and herbal tea bags. In hindsight, I don't know if it was the treats themselves that pleased us so much or the awareness that somebody cared about what we had been through.

The package we were most anxious to get, though, would have our travel papers inside it. For six long years after liberation, we waited patiently for a slip of paper inviting us to the United States of America. In the meantime, we studied. We worked. I made friends at the gymnasium. I (sort of) learned Hebrew. I learned to ignore bullies. I ate, and I grew to be a strong, healthy kid with a thick head of dark blond waves.

Mamishu became a pretty terrific hatmaker and expanded her talents to sewing women's corsets. To make ends meet, she continued occasional late-night runs to sell goods on the black market.

One afternoon in the winter of 1951, Frau Müller told us that a parcel had arrived for us while we were out. The oversized envelope contained the documentation for our visas and our tickets to New York City. We were to depart from the port city of Bremerhaven, Germany, boarding an American ship called the *General M. B. Stewart*—a military transport ship that would end up carrying 1,293 displaced persons to the country of our dreams. Mamishu held the papers up to the sky, her eyes raised to the heavens. Then she brought the stack of documents to her lips to kiss them.

Frau Müller was rarely affectionate, but she rushed to my mother and gave her a big hug, congratulating us both on the news. Our landlady would miss us, the Jews she eyed suspiciously at first but had grown to like.

"Well, *zeisele*. This is it," Mamishu said to me. She had tears of happiness streaking down her face, leaving a white line through her rouged cheeks. "There must be a song for this moment, but I'm so excited that words and rhymes escape me!"

To this day, that moment when I learned we would be coming to America is among the happiest moments of my life. On January 31, 1951—six years after I was liberated from Auschwitz, eleven years after I was born into a ghetto— my second life was about to begin.

33

THE BAR MITZVAH BOY

"**Wake up, Mamishu!**" I begged as I stood beside her bed. I knew she took forever to get ready, and I couldn't be late.

It was May 16, 1953, the day of my bar mitzvah—the Jewish ceremony for a thirteen-year-old boy marking his passage to adulthood. The clock said 5:10, but I was so nervous about reading my Torah portion that I was determined to arrive at synagogue early. I wanted to practice one more time with the rabbi.

Mamishu pulled up her covers and spoke to me without even opening her eyes. "Michael, there are four hours until services. The synagogue won't even be open for three. Go back to bed, *libling*."

I decided to let her sleep a little longer. "Okay, Mamishu," I said. "But remember that after today I won't be a *libling* anymore. By the end of the day, I'll be a man. So that means you have to give me a little more credit."

I was half kidding but also half serious. And I don't think I can exaggerate the amount of time it took for my mother to get ready in the morning. The way she put on her makeup, you'd think she was painting a van Gogh masterpiece. But she'd been through a lot, so I guess she deserved a little relaxation time in the mornings.

While she snoozed, I made myself breakfast in our small but clean two-room apartment at Ninety-Eighth Street and Madison Avenue in Manhattan. The kitchen was so narrow it barely fit two people side by side, but on that morning I had the two-by-four space all to myself.

I peeled open a soft, ripe orange, careful not to let any juice squirt onto my starched white button-down shirt. I thought about cooking two sunnyside-up eggs (my favorite) over the stove, but the risk seemed just too great. The last thing I needed was yellow yolk dripping down my new bar mitzvah suit!

Instead, I took my orange wedges and sat on the edge of the living room sofa, watching out the window as a surprising number of Saturday-morning early risers headed to work. We lived in a blue-collar neighborhood on the Upper East Side, where we were our own minority inside a larger minority community. Our neighbors were mostly Puerto Rican, and at five o'clock on a Saturday morning hardworking people heading to their jobs nodded as they passed hard-partying young people just coming home from dance halls and bars. We didn't quite fit, but this was home.

It had been just over two years since we'd crossed the Atlantic aboard the *General M. B. Stewart.* That was a journey I wish I could forget. Mamishu and I shared a tiny cabin with several other passengers on one of the lower decks of the slow-moving vessel. Along the way, I discovered that I get seasick on boats. Oh, my. I vomited for seven straight days.

By the time we reached the inspection station in New York, I was so weak my mother had to practically hold me up as we waited our turn in the customs line. I looked as bad as I felt. When we reached the front of the line, the customs officer told Mamishu I was too sick to enter the country and we would have to be returned to Europe. The U.S. government didn't want diseases from abroad to be carried to American citizens.

Mamishu begged and pleaded but didn't seem to be making any headway.

I had been studying English at nights in Munich for more than a year, and in my best accent I interrupted.

I remember clearly the exact words I spoke: "Sir, I am very healthy, I promise. I am only seasick. The waves were very rough at sea."

The man seemed taken aback at first. Then he smiled at me and said, "Nice English, kid. Welcome to the United States of America." He stamped my paperwork, and we were home.

Well, it wasn't quite that simple. We were home—but also homeless. My uncle David and aunt Gutia had offered to put a mattress on their dining room floor and had invited us to stay as long as we needed. But I was so sick that our first stop was the Hebrew Immigrant Aid Society. HIAS allowed Mamishu and me to stay at a facility on the Lower East Side of Manhattan near Orchard Street, where I could gain back my energy from severe dehydration and be monitored by doctors. We stayed there for maybe a week or even two. HIAS gave us three meals a day and new clothes to wear. That organization rescued us from what would otherwise have been a more harrowing arrival in a foreign land.

As soon as I was feeling better and Mamishu had gotten her bearings in New York, we moved straight in my uncle David's dining room floor. He pushed the heavy oak table into the living room, giving us enough space to share a mattress and two brown cardboard boxes for all of our clothes and toiletries.

Mamishu worked making corsets in her big sister's shop, called Agnes Malone. My aunt Ola—the one who had fled to Japan during the war—was the first of the Jonisch siblings to finally make it to America. It took her some time, and she leaned heavily on organizations like HIAS at first; but Ola ultimately found great success as an entrepreneur here. Mamishu made thirty dollars a week, and she supplemented that by taking odd babysitting jobs. She worked very hard and then came home at night to rest her head next to mine on a frameless mattress that lay where a dining room table should sit.

Uncle David was kind to share his Brooklyn rental with us, but I probably don't need to tell you how thrilling it was to finally learn that Mamishu had earned enough to rent her own apartment on Ninety-Eighth Street. I used Aunt Ola's address so I could enroll at Public School (PS) 6, one of the best public schools in New York. Mamishu wanted the finest schooling for me, even if it required a little sleight of hand.

Two years into my classes at PS 6, I still didn't have one single friend to formally invite to my bar mitzvah. I was never treated cruelly, but mostly felt invisible. I'm sure my classmates all considered me the weird kid with the funny accent and the strange tattoo on his forearm. They saw my numbers, no matter how hard I tried to keep them hidden. If I accidentally pushed my left sleeve up on a hot day, there it was: B-1148. It hurt to feel like a misfit, but I couldn't worry about that much. There wasn't time.

I got a job after school delivering prescription drugs for Feldman's Pharmacy on Ninety-Sixth and Madison Avenue, just two blocks from our apartment. The head pharmacist, Victor Oliver, became like a father to me. He taught me all about making compounds and how chemistry works to treat illnesses and save lives. The pay was fifty cents an hour. I saved up for nearly a year to buy Mamishu her first-ever black-and-white television set. I'll admit—I was pretty excited to watch TV, too.

And in what little time remained, I studied Torah with the rabbi so I could become a bar mitzvah.

Everyone was set to attend. Mamishu's four brothers arrived one by one, each of them shaking my hand at the door to the Park Avenue Synagogue like I was a real man.

Uncle Moniek and Uncle David had restarted their leather business, again, in the United States and it had taken off like gangbusters! Unfortunately, they left my Uncle Mullek out of their plans and he started his own leather business in Brooklyn. Uncle Mullek, too, was a success.

Aunt Ola wrapped me up in a big hug when she arrived, a cloud of citrusy perfume enveloping me. Her husband, my uncle Aleksander, pumped my hand. Uncle Aleksander had an import-export business and in the summertime, he let me pick up extra hours at his office, packaging items for shipment. He would never have missed my big day.

Aunt Hilda sent a letter of congratulations from Cuba, where she lived with her new husband, José Robinsky—a man who had fled Jewish persecution in Belarus a decade before the Holocaust. My aunt met José in Cuba and fell in love with him while she was waiting for her visa to the United States. We still all hoped she would move to New York one day, but she loved her life in Cuba.

Kristina-Ruth showed up to the Park Avenue Synagogue decked out like it was her wedding. She really does love to dress for occasions. She just went by Ruth now. Her little sister was there, too. Uncle Sam and Aunt Cecia had had another baby, Esther, born after the war in Munich and named for her grandmother. As they stepped through the doors into the sanctuary, my aunt and uncle let go of Esther's hands long enough to come and pat me on the back, saying, "*Mazel tov*—congratulations—dear Michael!"

Even Victor Oliver was there. The pharmacist who took the time to teach me about pharmacodynamics and molecular diagnostics also took the time to hear me read from the Torah.

One thing I'll never forget is the anonymous guest who

placed an envelope in my palm as he pumped my hand to congratulate me. I opened it after the ceremony. No note. But twenty-five dollars! I think I mentioned I made fifty cents an hour working at the drugstore. That gift took my breath away; it was a stranger's kindness that I'll remember forever.

As for Mamishu, she was late to my bar mitzvah. I told you so. She was still primping at quarter past eight when Aunt Cecia, knowing how anxious I was, came to the apartment to take me to the synagogue.

I knew Mamishu would be along soon, but I am embarrassed to say I cried when the rabbi told me we couldn't wait any longer—services had to begin. Just as I wiped my face with a tissue and stepped onto the *bimah*—the holy stage—the big wooden doors at the back of the room swung open and my mother came racing to the front row.

"Antshuldigt!" she mouthed to me in Yiddish. Sorry! Of course her makeup looked, well, overdone—and she was wearing a bright honey-colored dress and all her best jewelry. That included one very special wedding ring that would have had stories to tell, if it could have talked.

Mamishu blew a kiss at me from her seat. I couldn't stay mad at her.

During the ceremony, the rabbi raised a tiny silver kiddush cup I had brought to the temple with me that morning. He loudly chanted the prayer over the wine. The cup had one small ding on its side, but to every family member in the crowd it looked perfect.

When services ended, our big, bustling family crammed into the tiny living room of our apartment for a celebratory meal. Each holiday or religious milestone felt like a victory for every member of the family, and this one was filled with joy, that feeling every human craves and every survivor cherishes—the opposite of despair.

"Michael, my *libling*." My mother had pulled me aside to a quieter corner of the room.

"I'm not a *libling* anymore," I reminded her.

Mamishu nodded and then said with a grin, "Well, I suppose if you're not a child, then you're too old for presents, too, aren't you, big man?"

I laughed and told her of course I wasn't.

She gave me a gold watch, more valuable than anything I had ever owned in my life. She had been saving up for it since long before we came to America. Mamishu had dreamed about marking my bar mitzvah day with such a gift.

"Turn it over," she said.

I flipped the gold timepiece, my mouth agape with surprise and excitement. On the back was an inscription in bold letters: GAM ZE YA'AVOR.

"If you ever suffer hard times again, my darling—though I hope you never do—please turn your watch over and remember, this too shall pass."

Then she walked back to the center of the room to join the party, singing, singing like always, under her breath.

AFTERWORD BY MICHAEL BORNSTEIN

Many of the anecdotes gathered in this book came as a surprise—even to me—as my daughter and I researched and interviewed survivors who knew my family.

My father, Israel Bornstein, as the head of the Judenrat in the open ghetto of Żarki, is credited with saving hundreds of lives and, when possible, using his influential position to make conditions in the ghetto far more bearable.

Sadly, my father wasn't able to save his own son—my brother, Samuel—or himself. I don't remember either one of them. I wish I did. My portraits of both of them are based on family stories and countless conversations with many other people, starting with my mother.

My cousin Ruth lives in Florida now. The emotional scars of her early years—being twice ripped from her mother's arms—have never left her. She still remembers the day her parents returned for her at the church orphanage. She remembers the moment her mother, Cecia, sang to her in Hebrew and that dawning revelation that she had a real family. Ruth has three grown children. She also remains close to her little sister, Esther, born after the war.

Several years after she emigrated, my aunt Hilda married José Robinsky, the man she met in Cuba, and they had a baby girl named Estee. As she had in Poland, Hilda ignored signs of political conflict and stayed in Cuba long after it was safe. Once again though, she managed to escape. Two years after the Cuban Revolution, she packed two suitcases, one with clothes and one with photographs, and she traveled to Miami with her daughter. A month later, her husband managed to escape by boat, too. Estee married and gave Hilda two beautiful grandchildren, Andy and Allison. Estee did not learn her mother had been married before the war until after her mother's death. Hilda told her daughter often, "Just look forward. Always look forward."

In Miami, Hilda opened a women's clothing shop in South Beach. When my own children were little, we used to visit her there and she always treated my daughters to whatever scarves, headbands, or jewelry they picked out from the store. My aunt Hilda died in 1998.

My uncles re-created their leather business in America and found a great deal of success in New York. They are all gone now, the uncles and aunts, but they set the example for me of how a person can rebuild from nothing. Uncle

Moniek lost his wife and two children in the Holocaust, but he, like Aunt Hilda, found love again and remarried.

My aunt Ola, the one Jonisch family aunt who escaped Poland during the war, had been granted asylum in Japan by famed statesman Chiune Sugihara. She, too, made it to America along with her husband and daughter, Sylvia. Today, Sylvia and I are great friends—bonded by a unique family background and a rare understanding of how delicate and precious family ties can be.

As far as I know, my grandmother Dora never left Żarki. I do believe she found a permanent residence there, because years after our heavyhearted farewell, I regularly brought home heart medication from Feldman's Pharmacy in New York, which Mamishu, my mother, mailed to her in Żarki. Grandma Dora never did come to America.

Mamishu died in 1988 at the age of eighty-six. She was diagnosed with Alzheimer's disease, but, oddly enough, when the thieving illness stole her memory and her dignity it left behind the melody and lyrics to the ghetto song she sang to me as a child. Even from her nursing-home bed she loved to sing and would softly murmur, *"Zog nit keinmal als du gehnest dem letzen veg . . ."* Don't say this is your last journey. This is not your last path . . .

My mother remarried about seven years after we came to

America. Aunt Hilda set her up with one of José's friends from Cuba. His name was Chaim and he was a kind man. She moved to Cuba to be with him and then, years later, returned to the United States, settling in Florida, not far from Aunt Hilda. The sisters remained the best of friends.

Unlike Aunt Hilda, though, my mother talked constantly about my father and brother. Her heart never really healed from their loss, but she did try to focus on what was good in her life. She loved me with everything she had left to give.

As for me, I am not the awkward boy with the funny accent any longer. I know I mentioned that as a child in America, I had no friends. That was the truth. But just before the publication of this book, I got a surprise phone call from the reunion committee for my grade-school class at PS 6. They invited me to an event and I don't know why I decided to attend, exactly, but I did. Strangely, I found that sixty-five years after I first met those students, I now fit.

More than that, I was stunned that anyone remembered me at all. One former classmate sent my daughter Debbie an e-mail after the reunion saying she looked forward to reading *Survivors Club*. She told Debbie that she always remembered the boy who spoke little English and had "funny numbers" on his arm. She continued: "To this day I remember with shame that I have no memory of any teachers taking his classmates aside to explain what he'd been through . . . Clearly we would have been able to understand and perhaps been kinder in receiving him."

I do wish the same was true, but I am grateful this classmate and so many others welcomed me with open arms at the reunion. It is never too late.

I grew up to become a research scientist. I was accepted as an undergraduate student at Fordham University, but when my mother moved to Cuba to remarry during my freshman year, I was left homeless again. The nuns at the Catholic university offered to let me sleep in the infirmary, and once again an infirmary was my saving grace! People sometimes ask why my mother moved away for those years. I believe that in her mind, an eighteen-year-old was a grown man. She had given me the outlook and the tools to succeed, and she was ready to love again and be loved by my future stepfather, Chaim. She would never have left me in America if she did not feel I was ready to stand on my own.

Victor Oliver, that pharmacist from Feldman's drugstore, left an indelible imprint on my life. His early teachings sparked a genuine interest in science and chemistry. After college, I earned a PhD in pharmaceutics and analytical chemistry at the University of Iowa.

My greatest accomplishment at that university, though, was meeting a young woman named Judy Cohan, who would become my wife and the love of my life. Going on a blind date with her marked the second time in my life that luck saved me. Judy and I raised four children—Lori, Scott, Debbie, and Lisa—in a life filled with soccer games, birthday parties, and bliss.

One evening in the mid-1980s, Judy and I went with friends to see a movie called *The Chosen*. It is set in Brooklyn in 1945, and in one scene the two main characters watch a newsreel that shows children being liberated from Auschwitz. The movie director had used real footage from the liberation, and as I sat in my theater seat watching the screen I was in shock. I recognized my face in that footage, compiled from the movies taken by Soviet soldiers. I had never before seen the film or photographs of myself at Auschwitz.

Still, I continued to stay relatively silent about my childhood. My kids would ask, but my memories are slim of those days—a blessing and a curse. Also, I honestly like to focus on the positive. Just like Aunt Hilda, I look forward. I wanted my children to see and hear only about goodness.

Our four kids grew up and married incredible spouses of their own. They have collectively given Judy and me a brood of beloved grandchildren, now numbering twelve. Once again, our days are filled with soccer games and birthday parties—and an unyielding supply of that indescribable joy.

At our children's weddings and for grandbabies' bris or

baby namings, we have raised one very precious silver kiddush cup in gratitude and celebration. That family heirloom, once buried in my parents' backyard in Żarki, now stands as a symbol of a faith that can't be broken, no matter how great the test. Two generations after the Holocaust, from one survivor, there are four children and twelve grandchildren. There are hundreds of thousands more from other survivors and escapees. Hitler did not wipe out a religion. Today, our sense of identity is stronger than ever.

How do I know this? Shortly after *Survivors Club* was first published, I got an e-mail from a man who wrote that *he* is the boy standing behind me in the photo on the cover of the book. On the very same day, another e-mail appeared. A woman named Tova Friedman told me she was photographed alongside me, too. Tova knew of another survivor, Sarah Ludwig, a "girl" just my age now, who lives just miles from my New Jersey home and is standing directly to the left of me on the cover of this book. Sarah, Tova, and I reunited in June of 2017 as cameras from *NBC Nightly News* captured the moment. It could have been such a bleak morning. We all share such a ghastly past. But it wasn't that at all. It was a celebration of survival. With generations of children and grandchildren bouncing from the basement to the backyard of my daughter Debbie's home, we raised my family Kiddush cup and toasted to remembrance, tradition, prosperity, and happiness. As Sarah Ludwig later said, "We're all family now."

My cousins and kids tell me there is something different about me now, ever since I started sharing my past. They say I seem to be more at peace, and I don't think they're wrong. In fact, I surprised myself when Debbie asked if she could plan a family trip to Poland and I agreed to join. Sylvia, who fled Warsaw as a teen, came along. Aunt Hilda's daughter Estee and Ruth's daughter Yaffa bought tickets. In the days leading up to the trip, I wondered if it was a mistake. But there were surprises I could not have anticipated.

On the day we visited the site of the uprising in Warsaw, we ran straight into a group of ninety Israeli teens who learned I was a survivor. They asked me to tell my story and after I did, we spontaneously wrapped our arms around one another and began to sway, singing *"Yerushalayim Shel Zahav"* ("Jerusalem of Gold"), a song of hope in Hebrew. There, in the place where so many Jews died—dreaming of a free state—an Auschwitz survivor stood proud, alongside thriving teenagers from a free Israel. It was a moment I won't forget.

I also won't forget how my kids and cousins linked arms with me as we forced our feet to carry us under the infamous front gate at Auschwitz. We did what we came to do.

We said *Kaddish* for my brother and my father and for the one million Jews murdered there. My children bore witness. This was a difficult day for me.

In Żarki, where not one Jew now lives, the mayor set out an Israeli flag to welcome our group and surprised us with news that there would soon be a permanent exhibit to memorialize Jewish history in the town. We hope this will not be an empty promise. One year later, plans for a memorial are not advancing fast. Regardless, I found great peace from a discovery that came from the two women organizing that exhibit.

Shortly after *Survivors Club*'s first printing, British historian Lucia Morawska and Polish activist Karolina Jakoweńko reached out to Debbie and me. They had seen the book website and wanted to talk. I learned they had access to a treasure trove of never-before-shared photos snapped before, during, and after the war. In that secret cache, they found the only photo I have ever seen of my brother, Samuel. Sitting in a tree at a park near our home in Żarki, with my mother standing beside him, Samuel looked a lot like my own son and several of my grandchildren. The photograph is now included in the photo section of this book. It brings me great joy to know his face can't be forgotten now.

Recently, I retired from a long career in pharmaceutical research. In between ballet recitals and "Shabbat Child" visits to schools that my grandchildren attend, I've begun speaking regularly at schools, synagogues, churches, and museums around the country.

After one such talk, a man approached me. Saul Schulman told me he never attends Holocaust programs because it's too difficult, but for some reason he felt compelled to attend this one. He flew from Toronto, Canada, to Detroit, Michigan, to hear me and Debbie speak. It turns out Saul was hiding in the infirmary at Auschwitz-Birkenau, too. He was six years old, and I was four. We don't remember each other's faces, but like me, Saul survived because the Nazis never evacuated the infirmary. He told me he never speaks about Auschwitz himself, but he did share his story with us. I can understand his reluctance, of course. I hope one day Saul will join me, but for now I will keep talking. Wherever I go, I roll up my sleeve and show my tattoo. I tell kids as young as ten what happened to me as a child. When they grow up, their own children will probably never meet a survivor. My hope is that, one day, the students I reach will share my story with the next generation. I hope that readers are compelled to stand up against injustice, even when it doesn't affect them. I hope they are inspired to be kind to classmates who may be different. And above all else, I hope the world never forgets the victims of the Holocaust.

A BORNSTEIN FAMILY WHO'S WHO

Dora Bornstein: Mother to Israel Bornstein; Michael Bornstein's grandmother, whom he called Bobeshi (see glossary) or Grandma Dora. Dora remained with her grandson throughout the Holocaust and ultimately brought him safely back to Żarki, Poland, after the war's end.

Israel Bornstein: Michael Bornstein's father. As the head of the Żarki Judenrat, Israel was able to shield many of his family members from death and make conditions more bearable for numerous Jews during the Holocaust. Though his wife, Sophie, and his son Michael survived, Israel and his elder son, Samuel, both perished at Auschwitz.

Michael Bornstein: Born in the open ghetto of Żarki, Poland, on May 2, 1940, eight months after the German invasion; liberated from Auschwitz in 1945 as a four-year-old boy. After the war, Michael and his remaining family immigrated to the United States, where he earned a PhD and worked in pharmaceutical research. Today, Michael speaks at schools, sharing his experiences of the Holocaust.

Samuel Bornstein: Michael's older brother, who was murdered at Auschwitz in 1944. He died years before he reached the age of thirteen, the age required to become a bar mitzvah. On June 18, 2016, Michael's granddaughter Maddie chose to place an empty chair on the bimah as she became a bat mitzvah. That chair held a place for Samuel, the great-uncle Maddie never got to meet. She shared her blessings that day with him.

David Jonisch: Michael's uncle, married to Gutia. Michael and Sophie stayed with David and Gutia when they were getting settled in America following the war.

Sophie Jonisch Bornstein: Wife of Israel, mother of Samuel and Michael. Known by her children as Mamishu, Sophie protected Michael and survived the Holocaust. After the war, she worked making hats and corsets, eventually immigrating with Michael to America.

Esther Jonisch: Sophie's mother, Michael's grandmother. Esther taught Sophie to "always look forward." Sent to the Treblinka concentration camp when the ghetto in Żarki was cleared out, she perished there. Esther and her husband, Mordecai, had seven children: Ola, Sophie, Hilda, Moniek, David, Sam, and Mullek.

Hilda Jonisch: Sophie's younger sister. Hilda's first husband, Joseph Wygocka, left for America before the war, so Hilda stayed in Warsaw and worked at a bank. She was eventually sent to a series of several concentration camps and later to Buchenwald. After surviving the war, Hilda made her way to Cuba, where she married José Robinsky and had a daughter named Estee. Hilda and her family settled in America after the Cuban Revolution.

Ruth ("Kristina") Jonisch: Daughter of Cecia and Sam Jonisch, cousin of Michael. Ruth was born on August 1, 1939. When Sam and Cecia went into hiding, Ruth was taken in by a family friend and renamed Kristina. Later left outside a Catholic orphanage, she was raised by the nuns as a Catholic before being reunited with her parents following the war.

Mordecai Jonisch: Husband of Esther; father of Ola, Sophie, Hilda, Moniek, David, Sam, and Mullek; and grandfather of Samuel and Michael. Mordecai was killed at Treblinka along with Esther.

Ola Jonisch Hafftka: Sophie Bornstein's older sister. Ola escaped to Japan during the war with her husband, Aleksander, and their daughter, Sylvia. Japanese statesman Chiune Sugihara arranged for their immigration, and Ola and her family eventually came to America. Sophie worked in Ola's shop, Agnes Malone, when she and Michael arrived in New York.

Eli Zborowski: Kristina-Ruth's cousin and Michael's neighbor in Żarki survived in hiding during the war, along with his mother, sister, and brother. After the war, Eli met his wife, Diana, a fellow survivor, at a DP camp in Germany. Together, they immigrated to the United States, where Eli organized the first Yom Hashoah (Holocaust Remembrance Day) event in the United States in 1964 and established the world's first professorial chair in Holocaust studies at New York's Yeshiva University. He did work on the world stage to repair relations between Jews and Poles, meeting with leaders including Pope John Paul II, and he became chairman of the International and American Societies for Yad Vashem, Israel's Holocaust History Museum. An advocate, entrepreneur, husband, father, and grandfather, Eli Zborowski died in 2012 at the age of eighty-six.

Moshe Zborowski: Ruth's uncle. Moshe paid teachers so that the children in the Żarki ghetto could continue their schooling during the war. Moshe died trying to escape down the river just before the last Jews in Żarki were sent to concentration camps. His wife and three children survived, including Eli and Marvin Zborowski—who ultimately provided much information for this book. Marvin Zborowski says the Judenrat bribery scheme and Israel Bornstein saved his life when he was jailed in the ghetto for missing work, the incident mentioned in chapter seven.

A SURVIVORS CLUB PHOTO ALBUM

Sophie Jonisch Bornstein with Michael in Żarki, Poland, after the German invasion.

Michael's father, Israel Bornstein.

This image of Michael's brother, Samuel, alongside his mother, came to light shortly after the initial publication of *Survivors Club*.

Prewar photo of Żarki's main synagogue and adjoining square.

The Friday market in Żarki in the 1930s, with the Catholic church in the background.

Undated photograph from 1930s Żarki. From left: Unknown, Esther Jonisch, Hilda Jonisch Wygocka, possibly Joseph Wygocka (Hilda's first husband), and Sophie Jonisch Bornstein.

German invaders arriving in a bomb-damaged Polish village, September 1939.

Ruth's cousin Eli Zborowski (left) was photographed disguised as a woman on the streets of Żarki. He used this disguise regularly to sneak out of hiding and is pictured here alongside Jozef Kolacz, a farmer who helped to hide Eli and other relatives.

A group of Jewish men and older boys report for work inside the Żarki ghetto.

Even on his wedding day in 1942, Michael's uncle David Jonisch was forced to wear an armband identifying him as a Jew in Żarki. From left: David; his mother, Esther; and his bride, Gutia.

New arrivals at Auschwitz disembarking from the boxcars of the transport trains. On the horizon, the chimneys of two crematoria are visible to the left and right.

The selection process under way at Auschwitz in 1944, separating those chosen for slave labor and those who will be executed in the gas chambers.

A Kommando from the Kanada warehouse, wearing a striped uniform (right), stands near this group of women and children, ready to begin collecting the belongings the new arrivals will soon be forced to abandon.

A view of the Auschwitz gate in the foreground with the sign reading ARBEIT MACHT FREI (Work makes you free), as well as the electrified fences. In the background, a view of the kitchen barracks.

An aerial view of Auschwitz barracks, c. 1945.

An Auschwitz women's barracks in January 1945. Women slept three to a bed-shelf.

Soviet soldiers captured this image of Bobeshi, Michael's grandmother Dora (center), carrying him out of Auschwitz in 1945.

This image of Michael (at far right) and other child survivors of Auschwitz is another still from film footage taken days after their liberation in January 1945.

Michael and five other surviving family members photographed in Poland after the war. Top row: Cecia Jonisch, Sam Jonisch, and Sophie Jonisch Bornstein. Bottom row: Michael Bornstein, Hilda Jonisch, and Ruth Jonisch.

From left: Hilda Jonisch, Michael Bornstein, and Sophie Jonisch Bornstein, photographed together shortly after the war ended.

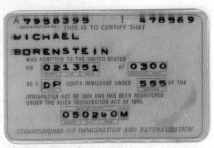

Undated photo of Michael, likely taken in Munich, Germany, in the late 1940s.

Michael's naturalization card, identifying him as a DP (displaced person). He arrived in America in 1951, essentially homeless.

Family members get together in New York City, May 1958. From left: Ruth Jonisch, Mullek Jonisch, Ola Jonisch Hafftka, and Michael Bornstein.

Some of the Survivors Club, plus fellow revelers, at a New York City family occasion in the early 1960s. Top row, from left: Michael Bornstein, Elsa and Mullek Jonisch. Top row, far right: David Jonisch. Bottom row, far left: Aleksander Hafftka. Bottom row, from right: Moniek Jonisch, Ola Jonisch Hafftka. Bottom row, center: Sophie Jonisch Bornstein.

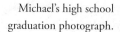

Michael's high school graduation photograph.

In college, Michael was allowed to sleep in the infirmary at Fordham University when the school learned he had no place to live.

Sophie Bornstein with her second husband, Chaim Nepomechie, in 1984.

Michael returned to Auschwitz for the first time in 2001 with his wife, Judy.

Michael in 2001 at the Żarki cemetery, the site of mass murders during the Holocaust.

Michael in 2015, speaking about his wartime experiences and showing his number tattoo.

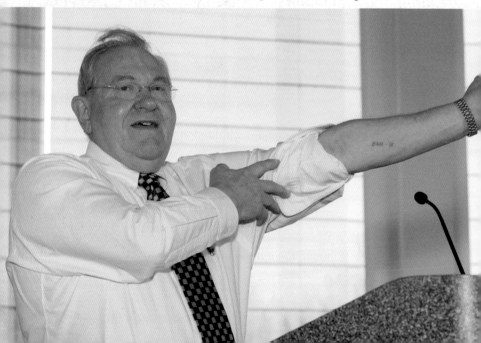

In June 2017, shortly after the first publication of *Survivors Club*, Michael was reunited with two child survivors, Tova Friedman (far left) and Sarah Ludwig, pictured alongside him in the iconic Soviet image taken after Auschwitz was liberated.

"We're all family now," Sarah Ludwig said after their emotional reunion.

Michael returned to Auschwitz with the support of many family members in September 2017.

Michael and Judy Bornstein surrounded by their four children, children's spouses, and twelve grandchildren, in the summer of 2018.

The Bornstein family kiddush cup, once buried underground in Żarki, Poland.

GLOSSARY

Allies: The alliance of nations fighting against Axis forces Germany, Italy, and Japan in World War II. The Allies included the United States, the United Kingdom, and the Soviet Union.

anti-Semitism: Hostility or discrimination toward Jews.

Auschwitz: The largest Nazi-run concentration camp, where more than one million prisoners died during World War II. It was located near the Polish town of Oświęcim.

Bobeshi: Yiddish for "Granny" or "Grandma."

Frau: German title meaning "missus."

gentile: A non-Jewish person.

Gestapo: An abbreviation for Geheime Staatspolizei (Secret State Police), the police force of Nazi Germany, which served in territories invaded by the Germans such as Żarki.

ghetto: An enclosed area where members of a minority group live, often involuntarily isolated from other parts of a town or city.

Herr: German title meaning "mister."

kosher: Meaning "clean" or "pure," describes food that is prepared following the rules of Jewish law.

Luftwaffe: The German air force.

Mamishu: A variant on the Yiddish endearment for "Mama."

rabbi: A Jewish religious leader.

rations: Fixed amounts of food given to citizens to combat food shortages during wartime.

Soviet Union: The nation formed by the union between communist Russia and other countries under its influence; it existed from 1922 to 1991.

SS: The abbreviation for Schutzstaffel (protective squadron), the paramilitary organization that enforced the Nazi Party's mission.

swastika: A hooked cross used as a symbol of the Nazi regime.

synagogue: A building used for Jewish religious worship.

Torah: The most holy book of the Jewish religion, outlining the laws of the faith.

Yiddish: The language spoken by many central and eastern European Jews; it is a hybrid of Hebrew and medieval German.

zloty: Polish currency.

Zyd: Polish term for a Jewish person.

NOTES ON SOURCES

In addition to Michael's own memories from this time period, we relied heavily on stories shared with us and other family members by Michael's mother, Sophie Bornstein. She told of forced contributions in Żarki, intimidation and thievery by Nazi guards, her efforts to save Michael's life at Auschwitz, and her astonishment at finding her youngest son had survived even after she was forced to leave him behind in the death camp. Her memory of being reunited with Michael in Żarki after the war was something she talked about often. She also described the shock of learning that the family's home was occupied by an interloper and that her only surviving son was living in a chicken coop. She was eternally grateful to her mother-in-law for keeping him alive.

Accounts by Michael's mother's sister, Hilda Jonisch Robinsky—including an audio recording made for the family on August 28, 1991—were also invaluable sources for this story. Hilda talked about her return to the Żarki ghetto, her escape from Warsaw, her survival at the Majdanek and Skarżysko camps, and her liberation from Buchenwald. Her return to Żarki, however, marked some of the most surprising moments of her life, she said—including her extraordinary conversation with the wagon driver related in chapter six.

We are very grateful to the family of a Żarki survivor who shared with us the private diary of his grandfather, who evaded deportation by hiding in a secret bunker from 1942 to 1945. This was an invaluable source of information about the treatment of Jews in the Żarki ghetto and the role Israel Bornstein played as Judenrat leader, and it lifted the veil on vague stories we knew about violent murders on Bloody Monday and in the days that followed the start of the war.

Another Żarki survivor, Marvin Zborowski, says he knew Michael's mother's family, the Jonisches, almost as well as he knew his own. Marvin, a voluminous source of information, generously shared stories about Michael's mother's and father's actions during the war. Marvin told us that he is among those whose lives were saved by Israel Bornstein. As mentioned in chapter seven, before the Żarki ghetto was liquidated, when a then-teenage Marvin was sentenced to be killed for missing a day of work, Israel bribed a Nazi official to secure Marvin's release. Marvin was there, too, when Michael's family members returned to Żarki one by one.

Marvin Zborowski gave testimony as part of the University of Southern California Shoah Foundation's project to collect and record Holocaust survivors' stories. That interview focuses on Marvin's own family's story, but it did include some important background on the invasion and liquidation of Żarki. The interview is available at youtube.com/watch?v=7Zd9Eh-5m6Y.

Eli Zborowski was a teenager when the war started. Decades later, his reflections on life before, during, and after the Holocaust in *A Life of Leadership—Eli Zborowski: From the Underground to Industry to Holocaust Remembrance* by Rochel and George Berman (Jersey City, N.J.: KTAV Publishing, 2011) provide an incredible picture of the oppression in Żarki. We relied heavily on this source to confirm stories shared by other relatives.

We are grateful to Margalit Edelson for helping us translate a collection of reminiscences by Żarki survivor Yakov Fischer that were published in Hebrew. Fischer knew Michael's father well and detailed his influence over a particular Nazi guard. He provided more information and confirmation of the Judenrat's bribery schemes and also described in great detail the events of Bloody Monday in Żarki. Fischer's essays are included in *Kehilat Żarki: Ayara be-Hayeha U-Ve-hilyona (The Destruction of Żarki)*, edited by Yitzhak Lador and published by former residents of Żarki in Tel Aviv, Israel, in 1959. A scan of the text is available at yizkor.nypl.org/index.php?id=1328.

At the Jewish Genealogy and Family Heritage Center in Warsaw, Poland, we were astounded to discover letters signed by Israel Bornstein in 1940 requesting aid for the ghetto.

The following sources provided key background on life at the Pionki labor camp that helped fill holes that Michael's mother's stories and Michael's own memories could not: videotaped testimony by survivors Sam and Regina Spiegel that is archived at the United States Holocaust Memorial Museum in Washington, D.C.; *Looking Back* by Mania Salinger (Northville, Mich.: Ferne, 2006); and the testimony of an unnamed Pionki survivor recorded in

Trelleborg, Sweden, on May 22, 1946, and archived at the Polish Research Institute at Lund University.

Ruth Jonisch Hart's survival story was well-documented and -remembered in a private diary and by survivors Eli and Marvin Zborowski, and we also learned many details from stories shared with the family over the years by Ruth herself, Cecia Jonisch, and Esther Jonisch Flint. We are honored to be documenting Ruth's remarkable survival in this book.

The following sources were critical in helping to provide additional background on life inside Auschwitz, including details about life for children, like Michael, who managed to escape the gas chambers. Michael does not recall exactly what he ate or how the barracks looked, for instance, so this information helped us build an accurate picture:

Dlugoborski, Waclaw, and Franciszek Piper, editors. *Auschwitz 1940–1945: Central Issues in the History of the Camp*, Volume 2. Translated by William Brand. (Auschwitz, Poland: Auschwitz-Birkenau State Museum, 2000).

Langer, Emily, and Ellen Belcher. "Sisters Live to Tell Their Holocaust Story," a lengthy article in the *Washington Post*, April 7, 2013.

Megargee, Geoffrey P., and Martin Dean, editors. *The United States Holocaust Memorial Museum Encyclopedia of Camps and*

Ghettos, 1933–1945, Volume II: Ghettos in German-Occupied Eastern Europe (Bloomington, Ind.: Indiana University Press, 2012).

Mozes Kor, Eva, and Lisa Rojany Buccieri. *Surviving the Angel of Death: The True Story of a Mengele Twin in Auschwitz* (Terre Haute, Ind.: Tanglewood, 2009).

Spector, Shmuel, and Geoffrey Wigoder, editors. *The Encyclopedia of Jewish Life Before and During the Holocaust.* Three volumes. (New York: New York University Press, 2001).

Finally, we wish to express our gratitude to many sources for permission to reproduce photographs from their collections:

Page x: *Michael with other children:* Courtesy of Państwowe Muzeum Auschwitz-Birkenau. Photo insert: *Samuel alongside his mother:* Jozief Bacior, courtesy of Brama Cukermana Foundation / *Żarki's main synagogue:* fotopolska.eu / *Jonisch family's leather-curing factory:* Courtesy of Sylvia Smoller / *Friday market in Żarki:* fotopolska.eu / *Undated photo from 1930s Żarki:* Courtesy of Sylvia Smoller / *German invaders:* Courtesy of ullstein bild/ Getty Images / *Eli Zborowski disguised as a woman:* Courtesy of Marvin Zborowski / *Jewish men report for work:* United States Holocaust Memorial Museum, courtesy of Leah Hammerstein Silverstein / *On his wedding day David Jonisch was forced to wear an armband:* Courtesy of Sylvia Smoller / *New arrivals at Auschwitz:* United States Holocaust Memorial Museum, courtesy of Yad Vashem / *Selection process under way:* United States Holocaust Memorial Museum, courtesy of Yad Vashem / *Group of women and children:* United States Holocaust Memorial Museum, courtesy of Yad Vashem / *View of the Auschwitz gate:* United States Holocaust Memorial Museum, courtesy of Instytut Pamięci Narodowej / *Aerial view of Auschwitz barracks:* United States Holocaust Memorial Museum, courtesy of National Archives and Records Administration, College Park / *An Auschwitz women's barracks:* United States Holocaust Memorial Museum, courtesy of National Archives and Records Administration, College Park / *Michael's grandmother Dora carrying him out of Auschwitz:* United States Holocaust Memorial Museum, courtesy of National Archives and Records Administration, College Park / *Michael and other child survivors:* United States Holocaust Memorial Museum, courtesy of Yad Vashem / *Hilda Jonisch, Michael, and Sophie Jonisch Bornstein:* Courtesy of Estee Pickens / *Michael in Munich:* Courtesy of Estee Pickens / *New York City family occasion in the early 1960s:* Courtesy of Sylvia Smoller / *Michael in 2015:* Courtesy of Bruce Challgren, PhotoPixels, LLC / *Michael and Judy Bornstein surrounded by their four children, children's spouses, and twelve grandchildren:* Courtesy of Tania Michel Photographie. Photographs not identified are from the collections of the authors.

ACKNOWLEDGMENTS

We may be a father-daughter writing team, but this book is truly the result of a whole-family effort. Judy Bornstein stayed awake until 3:00 a.m. too many nights, chasing down online leads for new information. Her research skills and tireless resolve are unmatched. Her love and guidance as a wife and mother are unmatched, too. Lori Bornstein Wolf never stopped encouraging us until the last page was complete, going far beyond the call of duty for a daughter and sister. Steve Holinstat finished his own long hours as an attorney by day and coached sports for three busy kids over the dinner hour, yet never turned down a request to edit and critique by night. And Lisa Bornstein Cohn and Scott Bornstein cheered on this project from day one. Marvin Zborowski is not quite a cousin, but we consider him family for life. He is one of the last Żarki survivors still alive, and he spent countless hours sharing information. There are no words to express our gratitude and our deep respect for this courageous, kind, and generous soul. Cousins Sylvia Smoller, Esther Flint, and Estee Pickens shared their photos and their wealth of knowledge. We are grateful to have a family like this in our lives.

Incredibly, finding an agent to guide us through this process turned out to be a family affair, too. We owe so much to our literary agent, Irene Goodman, but it's her *husband* we must thank first. Alex Kamaroff was sifting through his wife's teetering pile of submissions in late 2015. Something drew him to our sample chapters, and after he had read them, he told Irene, "Put down whatever you're doing. This is more important." Alex saw something special in our account, and for that we are eternally grateful.

Enter Irene Goodman. She asked us to send her the complete manuscript, and before she'd even finished it she called and told us straightaway that although some manuscripts never find a publisher, she wouldn't quit fighting for this one until her dying day. She is fierce, brilliant, kind, and protective, and we thank her for her tireless efforts.

Our editor at Farrar Straus Giroux, Wesley Adams, deserves another big thank-you. It is terrifying to entrust a virtual stranger with your own family's precious memories. Wes didn't just edit this book, he championed it from the moment Irene sent it his way. Wes pushed us to research more, dig deeper, and write smarter. For it to land in his care and that of his colleagues at the Macmillan Children's Publishing Group and at Macmillan Audio was a gift. From Farrar Straus Giroux Books for Young Readers editorial director Joy Peskin to copy chief Karla Reganold, copy editor Janet Renard, editorial assistant Megan

Abbate, and the marketing and publicity team of Mariel Dawson, Molly Brouillette, Lucy Del Priore, Morgan Dubin, Kathryn Little, and Jeremy Ross, we have been in the best possible hands. For all their help producing the updated paperback edition of this book, many thanks to Macmillan's Celeste Cass, Sophie Erb, Perry Minella, Val Otarod, Melissa Warten, and Ilana Worrell.

We also want to thank some unofficial, early editors—our friends who made time to screen our manuscript and give us feedback during the arduous writing process: Sara Wald, Allison Newman, Sue Hermans, Ed Decker, Ronna Scheckman, Ronna Wolf, Rabbi Sandy Sasso, and Barbara Shoup. Additionally, Margalit Edelson spent hours translating critical writings from Hebrew to help us uncover more family background, and she put her heart into the project alongside us. Veteran author Sarah Mlynowski got us to the start line, encouraging the writing process and introducing us to colleagues in the publishing world.

We appreciate the assistance of Yad Vashem in Israel for providing us with documents and invaluable research. We also wish to thank the United States Holocaust Memorial Museum for their help with photographs, although the views or opinions expressed in this book, and the context in which the images are used, do not necessarily reflect the views or policy of, nor imply endorsement by, the museum.

Finally, Michael in particular would like to acknowledge Judy Bornstein for being an endlessly patient wife who travels to every single speaking engagement, making sure that PowerPoint presentations work and Wi-Fi connections hold. She coordinates and juggles, and her ever-present support makes everything in life better.

Debbie would like to send a special acknowledgment to her husband, Steve, and their three children, Jack, Katie, and Ellie, who loved her even when her head was buried in her laptop, fingers banging away at the keys, while she tried to finish this project. And finally, she wishes to thank her own father for entrusting her with helping to write *Survivors Club*. She considers this collaboration to be the most important piece of work of her professional life.